Advanced
Backstabbing and
Mudslinging Techniques

D1157631

George Hayduke's

Advanced Backstabbing and Mudslinging Techniques

A Lyle Stuart Book
Published by Carol Publishing Group

First Carol Publishing Group Edition 1991

Previously published under the title:
*Payback! Advanced Backstabbing and
Mudslinging Techniques*

A Lyle Stuart Book
Published by Carol Publishing Group

Editorial Offices   Sales & Distribution Offices
600 Madison Avenue   120 Enterprise Ave.
New York, NY 10022   Secaucus, NJ 07094

In Canada: Musson Book Company
A division of General Publishing Co. Limited
Don Mills, Ontario

Lyle Stuart is a registered trademark of
Carol Communications, Inc.

Manufactured in the United States of America
ISBN 0-8184-0560-0

10 9 8 7 6 5 4 3 2 1

Carol Publishing Group books are available at special discounts
for bulk purchases, for sales promotions, fund raising, or
educational purposes. Special editions can also be created to
specifications. For details contact: Special Sales Department,
Carol Publishing Group, 120 Enterprise Ave., Secaucus, NJ 07094

Neither the author nor the publisher assumes any
responsibility for the use or misuse of information
contained in this book

DEDICATION

Of all my friends, gentle critics, and supporters, none has been a bigger inspiration and pathfinder for me than Dr. Park Elliott Dietz, M.D., M.P.H., Ph.D., who has caused me to shuffle my feet in childlike embarrassment and say "ahh, shucks" to the delightful reviews he has given my books in the professional tomes whose reputations he heightens by his inclusion in their pages.

So, as we crude, boorish cretins with far fewer letters after our names say in our own unwashed, uncredentialed way, "Park, baby, this book's for you."

With humor and absolute disrespect, I wish to dedicate this book to the memory of Johnny and Barby, with my surprise to learn that they don't yet have a his & hers salt lick in their cozy office.

CONTENTS

INTRODUCTION

The talk show caller was astounded, I was semi-embarrassed, and Danny Wright was laughing. It was the drought summer of 1988, and the nice folks at 3WE-radio, Danny, Ken Kennan, and Susanne Hammer, had just titled me, "The Dirty Harry of Literati." A lot of time has passed by since then, and the title fits no more comfortably today than it did back then.

Barry Young of KFYI radio in Phoenix, which is almost my home station by now, said about me being on his show, "No other station in the valley brings you such a high standard of tasteful community service." I was thrilled, touched, and chilled to the point of a tear leaking from my life-toughened eye.

Radio talk shows are not only fun, they're also educational. Many hosts are astounded to find so much positive and humorous audience reaction to my ideas of getting back at life's bullies. There's a real grassroots rebellion out there. By contrast, the media stars and our elected things who live inside the beltway moat that protects us from Fortress Washington don't know much about this rebellion.

It is just absolutely impossible to walk high enough and wide enough to step over the mountain of repressive shit pouring out of the nation's anus, Washington, D.C. And, as our beloved democracy continues to crumble under the heel of increasing police-state politics—a process begun by Richard Nixon, championed by Ronald Reagan, and faithfully allowed by George Bush—repression grows. Consider the flurry of preplanned gun control of 1989 and

1

the flag-burning nonsense. I don't know who sickens me more, a flag burner or the super asshole politician who takes advantage of patriotic blindness.

But, as every good Hayduker knows, any repressive society offers vast opportunities for excitement, humor, and payback for those willing to assume minor risks on behalf of freedom and the repressed.

For too many people, resignation to all of that repression is the lock on their lives. The ideas and the fun in my books are the key that will open that repressive lock. The tumblers of that lock of repression also respond to the picks of humor, satire, and irony.

Indeed, the great power of irony is its subtle and lasting effect. My idea is to lightly etch a lasting scar on your mark's memory (rather than the direct force of blunt, troglodyte trauma). Not everyone agrees with my way of payback, though.

For example, all of my friends from the Hand-Wringing Society of America are starting their nasal whine about LAW, COURTS, THE SYSTEM, THE RATIONALITY OF THE HUMAN ORDER, and the second most insidious lie of the late twentieth century, "Gee, The System really works!" Yeah, well monkey muffins to that bullshit. It works only if you're rich and powerful or control those who are.

Our laws, as written and practiced today, are a lottery depending upon chance, circumstance, power and the frailty of human whim. Don't rely on the laws and the judges who interpret them. To be sure, some judges are humane and pragmatic, while others consider themselves deity and still others are merely gutter politicians wearing black robes. Our laws are as useful or useless as the Ten Commandments, depending upon how much faith you have, how much loot you can offer, and how far truth can be separated from fact. Most powerful people are very critical of Haydukery.

Some of these moral eunuchs whine that Hayduking is destructive. If taken seriously, it might be. But, consider what someone else said, someone whose sense of fair play and justice is more American to me than all of those whiners—Auntie Em.

Auntie Em says, "I see destruction of living ecosystems as violence, and yet, the actions taken against that violence as *accelerated recycling*. It is important that the elements removed from our earth to build machines, for example, be returned. Accelerated recycling moves this process along."

What dear old Auntie Em meant, for example, was that an earth mover is made of steel, which comes from iron ore, which comes from the earth. I am sure you can extend this logic to fit her philosophy of accelerated recycling.

Some readers may find this logic to be the height of cynicism. I'm not so certain. Yet, one reviewer said I was the ultimate cynic and probably a failed idealist. She was half correct. I have never been an idealist. Please, no sword is bloodier than that of an idealist who feels his morals or his ethics have been betrayed. However, there are some folks who say that a cynic is a failed moralist. I am not one of them, either.

Am I really a Dirty Harry? Nah, not even close . . . . I'm a sweetheart. A gentle, middle-aged old duffer who's seen too much for too long to be truly mean. I'll turn all four cheeks before you even get my attention. After that, well, the user-friendly light gets switched off.

My friend Blatta Hooyek once toasted me at a banquet, saying, "George has the power to make bullies pee when their bladders are dry, to make them vomit deep bile when

3

they're not sick, and to make them pump blood when they have no cuts."

For any person who's been badly burned by a bully of any stripe or institution, my ideas of revenge are a very sweet and soothing salve. But be careful in your quest to fight fire with fire—or salve, for that matter. Remember, the fire department fights fire with water. Or, as William Shakespeare, alleged author of the Nancy Drew mystery books, once wrote, "Heat not a furnace for your foe so hot that it do singe thyself."

Happy entertainment purposes only (i.e., good reading and good hunting, friends). Remember, this is all in fun, all in fun.

George W. Hayduke
Cacahuates, Panama
October 1989

GENERAL ADVICE

Throughout this book I make universal reference to the "mark," which is a street label hung on the victim, male or female, of a scam or con or act of vengeance. In our case, the mark is a bully—anyone or anything—who has done something unpleasant, foul, or unforgivable to you, your family, your property, or your friends. Never think of a mark as the victim of dirty tricks. Think of the mark as a very deserving bully, a target of your revenge.

Before you study any of the specific sections of this book, read these next few vital paragraphs. They tell you how to prepare before going into action.

1. Prepare a plan.

Plan all details before you take action at all. Don't even ad-lib something from this book without a plan of exactly what you're going to do and how. If your campaign involves a series of actions, make a chronological chart (don't forget to destroy it when you're through), and then coordinate your efforts. Make a list of possible problems. Plan what you'll do if you get caught—depending upon who catches you. You must have every option, contingency, action, reaction, and evaluation planned in advance. Remember, time is usually on the side of the trickster. As Winston Churchill—who is one of my favorite heroes for many, many reasons—once said, "A lie gets halfway around the world before the truth even puts on its boots." Or, as that old Sicilian homily goes, "Revenge is a dish best served cold," which means don't strike while your ire is hot. Wait. Plan. Think. Learn.

2. Gather intelligence.

Do what a real intelligence operative would do and compile a file on your mark. How detailed and thorough you are depends upon your plans for the mark. For a simple get even number, you obviously need less inside information than if you're planning an involved, time-release campaign. Before you start spying, make a written list of all the important things you need to know about the target—be it a person, company, or institution.

3. Buy away from home.

Any supplies, materials, or services you need must be purchased away from where you live. Buy far in advance and pay in cash. Try to be as inconspicuous and colorless as possible. Don't talk unnecessarily with people. The best rule here is the spy's favorite—a good operative will get lost in a crowd of one. The idea is for people not to remember you.

4. Never tip your hand.

Don't get cocky, cute 'n clever, and start dropping hints about who's doing what to whom. I know that may sound stupid, but some would-be tricksters *are* gabby. Of course, in some of the cases this will not apply (e.g., unselling car customers at the dealership, or other tricks in which the scenario demands you personal involvement).

5. Never admit anything.

If accused, act shocked, hurt, outraged, or amused, whichever seems appropriate. Deny everything, unless, again, your plan involves overt personal involvement. If you're working covert, stay that way. The only cool guy out of Watergate was G. Gordon Liddy; he kept his mouth shut.

6. Never apologize; it's a sign of weakness.

Normally, harassment of a citizen is a low-priority case with the police. The priority increases along with the mark's socioeconomic status in the community and with his or her political connections. If you are at war with a corporation, utility, or institution, that's a different ball game. They often have private security people, sometimes retired federal or state investigators. By habit, these people may not play according to the law. If you play dirty tricks upon a governmental body, prepare to have a case opened. But how hard it is followed depends upon a lot of factors. Understanding all this ahead of time is part of your intelligence planning before you get started.

THE ELEVEN COMMANDMENTS OF REVENGE

Thanks to my Apostle of Revenge, Dick Smegma, I humbly present for your perusal, belief, and adherence, the Eleven Commandments of Revenge. Stay faithful and you'll enjoy a lot of yucks without suffering the heartbreak of being caught.

1. *Thou shalt neither trust nor confide in anyone!* If you do, that person could eventually betray you. Even if it is a relative or spouse, don't tell anybody what you are up to. Implicated accomplices are OK.

2. *Thou shalt never use thy own telephone for revenge business!*
   Always use a public telephone or that of an unwitting mark so calls cannot be traced back to you or to someone who knows you.

3. *Thou shalt not touch revenge documents with thy bare hands!*
   Bare hands leave fingerprints! Wear gloves.

4. *Thou shalt become a garbage collector!* Once your victim places his trash outside his home/office for pickup, it is legal for you to pick it up yourself. You can learn a lot about your mark by sifting through his

papers and such. The pros do it all the time.

5. *Thou shalt bide thy time before activating a revenge plot!*
Give the victim time to forget about you and what he's done to wrong you. Getting even too soon makes it easier for him to discover who's doing it!

6. *Thou shalt secure a "mail drop" address in another city!*
You don't want revenge mail being traced back to your residence/home, do you?

7. *Thou shalt learn everything there is to know about thy victim!*
The best revenge schemes/plans are hatched by people who know their victims better than their victims know themselves.

8. *Thou shalt pay cash all the time in a revenge plot!*
Checks, money orders, etc., can be traced back to you. Cash cannot!

9. *Thou shalt trade with merchants who have never heard of you!*
Do business with people only once when involved in a revenge plot. You can wear a disguise so the people you are involved with will have trouble identifying you in a legal confrontation.

10. *Thou shalt never threaten thy intended victim!* Why warn your intended victim that you are going to get even? When bad things begin to happen to your victim,

whether or not you caused them, your victim will remember your threat, and he or she will set out to even the score with you.

11. *Thou shalt not leave evidence lying around, however circumstantial!*
    If you are thought to be actively engaged in having fun at your mark's expense, the authorities may visit you. Thus, it would be prudent not to have any books by Hayduke or Chunder at home or in the office. Note well what Rochefoucauld wrote in *Maximes*, "The height of cleverness is to be able to conceal it."

HOW TO USE
THIS BOOK

I have arranged these subjects by method and mark, listing them alphabetically. In addition to using the obvious subject headings, you can also do a cross-reference of your own. Or you can adapt a method listed for one mark for another mark or situation. This book is as versatile as your own imagination.

While this mix 'n match versatility is standard, the personalized nasty touch is still the best. Another effective part of this business is the anticipation of further damage after your initial attack. This is grand psychological warfare.

This entire concept reminds me of what Ralph Waldo Emerson said about a weed, "And what is a weed? It's a plant whose virtues have not yet been discovered."

CAUTION

The schemes, tricks, scams, stunts, cons, and scenarios presented here are for information and amusement purposes only. It is not my intent that you use this book as a manual or trickster's cookbook. I certainly don't expect that anyone who reads this book would actually ever *do* any of the things described here. This book is written solely to entertain and inform readers, not to instruct or persuade anyone to commit any unpleasant or illegal act. Given my own mild disposition, I could hardly tell someone else to make any of these tactics operational.

Consider the case of mistaken vengeance that took place in Vienna, Austria, in 1985, when Leopold Renner thought his wife was cheating on him because he saw her holding hands with another man. The shocked husband stuffed twenty-seven of her live, exotic pets—one after another—into the churning garbage disposal. Down went screaming parakeets, hamsters, mice, and tarsiers into a gushy gruel feeding into the sewage drains.

Fact: His wife Frieda was holding the hand of her brother, whom she had not seen in a dozen years, and was bringing him home to meet her husband. True story.

A good Hayduker works smart and covers all of the angles. Plan for all options and all contingencies. And remember this worthy advice from J.R.R. Tolkien, "It doesn't do to leave a live dragon out of your calculations if you live near him."

IN MEMORIUM

As many of you know, Ed Abbey was my sometimes unwilling mentor and the man who gave me literary life. Ed Abbey died early in 1989 at the far-too-young age of sixty-one. Dave Foreman, one of his closest friends and a man whose ethics and actions bring a ton of respect to humanity, wrote a proper sentiment about Ed Abbey. Here, with Dave Foreman's gracious permission, is that sentiment.

*****

March 20, 1989. I'm sitting in a cheap motel room somewhere in the unzoned international airport district of Houston, Texas. We are swallowed by a national monument to free enterprise. Nancy and I have just returned from Belize, where we spent ten days snorkeling and bird watching, exploring the interface of coral reef and tropical rainforest, studying the destruction and the protection of Central America. I'm coughing up fat, green lungers. The Caribbean Sea waged a dreadful assault on my sinuses. Nancy, the nurse, is worried. She thinks I may have pneumonia. "As soon as we're back in Tucson, you're going to see Herb," she nags. I nod a resignation to let her take me to my doctor, with whom I've become too well-acquainted thanks to a Brown Recluse Spider bite last fall.

While I concentrate on a particularly nasty glob somewhere down in my bronchial tubes, Nancy calls the *Earth First! Journal* office in Tucson to let John Davis know we're back in the States. I know as soon as the hellos are

13

said. Nancy's face is grey. John isn't known for his delicacy.

Ed Abbey is dead.

It's as though the last redwood has been cut down. It's as though the Grand Canyon has been dammed. It's like a monstrous oil spill in Prince William Sound.

Sitting on the bed in the Houston motel room, I remember eleven days earlier, the night before Nancy and I were to leave on our long-planned trip to Belize. We're at the *Earth First!* office in Tucson for a local EF! meeting. The phone rings. It's Clarke Abbey. "Dave, could you come over? He's bleeding again."

Nancy and I jump in the car, dash across the Santa Cruz River, nearly get lost (the eternal construction of Tucson has torn up the road by Abbey's house). Ed's in the bathroom. He passes out. Nancy and I carry him to our car. Doug and Lisa Peacock arrive. Lisa takes the kid. Doug and Clarke follow us in Doug's car. Flashing blinkers, weaving in and out of traffic, pushing red lights, I'm trying to get Ed to the hospital. Nancy monitors his pulse. She warns me, "The last thing we need is a car wreck. He's hanging in there. Slow down."

Outside the emergency room, Peacock and I smoke a cheap cigar and drink warm beer. The strong ones, Nancy and Clarke, are inside. Two hours later, Ed is in intensive care. Nancy and I divide the night—she'll take the first shift until 3 A.M.; then I'll come in.

I sit in intensive care, in the semidarkness of Ed's room, watching him sleep. Heart monitor. Tubes in his veins. Constant attention from the critical-care nurses. Is this where Ed Abbey belongs? Is this where he should die? *Why have I brought him here?* The author of *Desert Solitaire*, here in this temple of technology, this ultimate expression

14

of our alienation from the food chain? Could I have ever dreamed this insanely ironic moment in 1971 when I first read *Desert Solitaire*? Maybe it's not happening. It can't be happening. It's a nightmare, an acid flashback.

Did I do the right thing? Should I have instead driven West? Out to Papago Well, Ajo Peak, across the border to Elegante Crater, the Gran Desierto? That's where we belong. Not here.

But even this night passes.

In the morning, Ed's awake, but weak. We talk. He wants to know my opinion on the operation—the portal shunt—the only thing that can save him. I encourage him to do it. Nancy—always the critical-care nurse—returns and explains it to him. Ed trusts this strong woman, my wife. He's a good judge of character. She encourages him.

Tests determine that the necessary vein for the shunt exists. Nancy and Clarke talk about it in the corridor. Ed is wheeled by. He and I grip hands and look eye-to-eye. And then Nancy and I leave to catch a plane. To Houston for the night, then on to Belize. The next morning from Houston, Nancy calls the hospital and talks to the nurses. The operation was a success. Our guilt evaporates. We enjoy Belize.

Back in Houston, the guilt returns. I took him to the hospital. I helped talk him into the operation. Is it my fault that he died hooked up to machines in a sterile hospital instead of in the desert?

Except for a splitting sinus headache, I'm a zombie on the flight to Tucson. After landing, we hear the good news. The operation *was* a success. What killed Ed was a complication a couple of days later. But the operation bought him time—time to go home, time to sit in the desert, time to die in peace at night in his study, alone with the cries of coyotes, free from the science fiction technology of the

15

intensive care unit. Time to die like a man, like an animal. With dignity.

At the wake the next morning I am thankful for my sunglasses. They hide my red, puffy eyes. Chuck Bowden and Jack Dykinga try to talk to me. I croak out a reply beneath my damp cheeks. Chuck mumbles and says we'll talk later, then stumbles off. It's only nine o'clock in the morning, but the beer and wine and tequilla and Jack Damage are flowing at Sus Picnic Area, Saguaro National Monument West Unit. Desert rats, monkeywrenchers, Park Service employees, literati . . . the eclectic world of Ed Abbey has come to say goodbye and carry out his last wishes.

I realize how important ritual is, how necessary it is for journeying through one's grief at a time like this. Susie Abbey, 20 years old, with a different hair color than the last time I saw her, is reading something on anarchy that her father wrote. I envy her strength, her clear voice, her straight carriage. It's obvious whose daughter she is. I look at Clarke. How is he able to hold up through this? Susie finishes. Clarke rises, turns to the desert and yells, "Jack, go for it!" From far out in the desert, Jack Loeffler plays taps on his trumpet. My beer tastes of hot salt. Is it anguish or a pneumonic cough that's got hold of my lungs?

With the dying notes of Jack's trumpet, with the draining of that salty beer, with the retching up and spitting out of something from deep in my lungs — the grief is gone. Cried out. Now it is time to talk and laugh and drink and swap Ed Abbey stories. The rumor makes its rounds through the celebrating crowd: Ed is in the desert. No preservatives, no packaging. He's home. We eat fresh poached cow, smoke cigars, and drink. Howie and Marilyn stroll off to a sandy wash to carry out Abbey's instructions

16

for his wake. Somebody fires a pistol.

Some few people walk large in life. With death they leave new myths, new archetypes. Edward Abbey was one of these, one of the few in this decadent century to walk with primal dignity. As I watched him in the intensive care unit through that long night, I marveled at his poise. Unconscious on drugs, plugged into a heart monitor, plumbed with IV tubing, he still had the self-confidence, the integrity, the nobility of an animal. Here was no nihilist, no existential victim of the banality of modernism. No, here was a man who had lived and was unafraid to die. He died as he lived: without apology, without excuses, without pandering.

In his death, Abbey joined a small company. Perhaps only Henry David Thoreau, John Muir, Aldo Leopold and Rachel Carson have touched so many souls so profoundly with the message of the wilderness. Ed Abbey was a great man because he articulated the passion and wisdom of those of us who love the wild. He was a spokesperson for our generation and for generations to come of those of us who understand where the real world is.

He also joined Mark Twain and H.L. Mencken in wielding a rapier-like pen to prick the inflated egos of those who take themselves too seriously. The self-righteous humanists who hated Abbey never understood what he was saying. It is their loss.

And for those of us who understood the words of Edward Abbey, those words carved for all time in the sandstone bedrock of the desert, it is our joy that he lived and spoke so eloquently that which we so deeply feel.

We cannot replace such a man. None of us can emulate him or fill his shoes. But we can continue the work that we shared with him. His life, like each of his books, is a rock.

17

A piece of sandstone that fits comfortably in the hand. You know what to do with it. He told you.

ADVERTISING

As I've written in each of my books, advertising can be a wonderful little helper when you want to lampoon someone. Let me share some vignettes with you. This first one was suggested by someone we'll call Hubert Gewgaws, who had been "Dear-Huberted" by some tart who liked money more than love.

Hubert thought about running some classified and small display ads in the local campus newspaper and in one published for the funky streetfolk. Naturally, each ad would carry the name, address, and work telephone number of his former friend. I suggested he also run some of the ads with her sugar daddy's work number. Here are some examples of his ad copy:

• WELL-USED VIBRATOR WANTED by lonely, horny lady. Prefer one with kinky stains. Contact . . .

• SOILED PANTIES NEEDED FOR PSYCHOLOGY EXPERIMENT . . .

• I WILL SHARE EXPLOSIVE DIARRHEA AT YOUR NEXT PARTY. Call for details . . .

• THREE GENERATIONS OF MUTUAL MASTURBATION ON VHS. Daughter, mom, and grandma . . .

I also thought he might design a flyer to plaster on car windshields at local shopping malls. It would feature a photo of the nasty lady along with this headline: "WARNING!! This woman's vagina has tested positive for radon . . . . Avoid her at all costs. Call public health officials and the DEA!" I have no idea if he used this idea or not. In all

19

fairness, though, he should have. The woman had knowingly devastated both his bank account and his heart.

Tommie Titmouse also uses ads to tweak the beaks of marks and of our moral thought police. He uses those shopper newspapers that run private citizen classified advertising on a "no-sell, no-pay" basis. Here are a few ideas from Tommie's delightfully creative mind:

• Run an ad selling your mark's Harley at about two-thirds of the going price. The mark will be visited by big bikers who might not have a sense of humor about all this. With luck, they'll dance the salsa on his testicles.

• If, in addition to being deserving, your mark's a real geek and/or married to the ultimate bitch/bastard, you can advertise his or her porno collection for sale. Be sure to mention that the collection includes family, neighbors, pets, and friends starring in amateur videos of orgies, etc. Offer free previews, and provide your mark's address and telephone number.

• Perhaps your mark is one of those ban-the-gun assholes who is so intelligent as to fail to understand the Second Amendment. You could run ads selling the mark's gun collection, including fully automatic weapons. This will get the attention of the Feds very quickly.

The point here is to create situations in which the mark is forced to deal with the likes of people he doesn't even want to know about, much less meet in unpleasant circumstances.

AIRLINES

If they stay in the air the entire flight and fall back to earth in a controlled fashion, most airline flights these days are both smooth and safe, although rarely on time. So it is also rare that anyone needs to use the little motion sickness bags for their original, intended purpose. That gives me a fine idea for you.

Gather up these handy little containers when you deplane at your final destination. These receptacles make magnificent containers for previously owned animal body parts, overripe pieces of chicken, or fecal matter that you'll soon be sharing with your mark. The secret is to seal the smelly little surprise in the bag, then figure the most appropriate (which may not mean quick) delivery system.

As Sandra Sitzbath says, "Nothing says lovin' like something from the oven . . . or the lab . . . or the roadway . . . or the latrine."

ANSWERING MACHINES

If you've been bugged by those electronic sales machines that call to annoy you at home when you're doing something else (the assholes call this bothersome technique "telemarketing"), here is an interesting new response. Most of us just hang up or respond with expletives when the recorded voice asks for our reply.

Carla Savage has another approach. She asks—rather rhetorically, of course—"What might happen if you don't hang up?"

"I don't need my phone to be free at night," Carla explains. "So I just set it down when one of the recorded sales voices calls. What happens? Does the tape loop play over and over? Does it automatically disconnect? Does it shut down their system?"

Gee, Carla, quality telephone time is such a terrible thing to waste, and I'm happy to see you turn their money into your time. This is a grand idea, and it explains how much more civilized Carla is than I. The next time I meet someone who tells me that he or she is in "telemarketing," I'm going to blow my nose on that person.

ART

This tidbit of art history comes to us from Mad Man Mike—a true Renaissance man—who talks of Michelangelo, an artist of some reputation. According to Mad Man Mike, the other Mike (Michelangelo) was a Renaissance Hayduker as well.

Mad Man Mike says that when Michelangelo painted *The Last Judgment*, he used the faces of real people in his art. One such subject was Biagio de Cesena, who was Pope Paul III's master of ceremonies as well as Michelangelo's mark.

"The great painter put Biagio's face on one of the demons, before whom a boatload of lost souls was parading. The demon's name was Minos, and he appears at the lower righthand corner of the painting," Mad Man Mike relates.

The fun began when Biagio was told of the likeness and begged the pope to order Michelangelo to change the face on the painting. The pope, a great believer in mystics (how else could he have gotten to be pope), refused, saying that not even a pope could rescue the damned from hell. Biagio was horrified and thought he'd been cursed. His life went quickly downhill from that point.

How can you utilize this bit of culture? Simple. Include your mark in paintings and photos. I have a friend back East who makes composite photos putting mark faces on different bodies, including nonhuman ones. He then creates

23

posters or postcards and circulates them. Get the idea?

AUTOMOBILES

The sources for many of these stunts would make interesting books of their own. I got the following bit of information from my old buddy Grizzled, but I'd heard of the same trick earlier from a former military colleague, who, at last shadow, was doing some analytical consulting for one of America's unlisted alphabet soup agencies.

My friend was taught how to do it by government employees at some farm in Virginia. (You know the sense of humor of these rural rustics.) Both men told me the effect is loud, spectacular, and potentially quite dangerous. It is also, obviously, very destructive.

Here's what you do. Remove a spark plug from your mark's automobile. Add a quarter cup of black powder (the type used in muzzleloaders) to one of the cylinders by pouring it through the spark plug hole. Replace the plug.

According to the professionals, when the mark turns the ignition key, the second sound heard will be a loud, frightened expletive. Both men indicated that this stunt will easily trash an engine and could cause damage to the radiator, battery, and more.

I asked my old army pal if he'd ever done it for real. He looked at me as if I were eleven years old and said, "Uncle *paid* me to do it!"

Yeah, I remember. And for those of you who don't, the same thing is detailed in a Special Forces manual I recall from long, long ago. So, please don't blame me. We sure do live in a double-cross world, don't we?

Speaking of auto abuse, I was reading a letter from the Sperminator that mentioned another old "disablement" trick from a military manual. In this one, a pint of raw linseed oil is added to the vehicle's gasoline tank.

The extreme heat in the cylinders will cause the linseed oil to break down into a very sticky resin that will eventually stop the engine from running. This could take several hours or two days, depending upon circumstances. And, as I said, you can join me in thanking The Sperminator for his good memory and then credit the U.S. Army for the gig.

Willy Thornton's family was having problems sleeping because a nearby neighbor's kid had a car with, essentially, a nonmuffler. It began life as a Hollywood muffler, and even that wore out. Now the kid's car sounded like a crop-dusting airplane.

After many complaints from the Thorntons, the parents forced the kid to get a new muffler. To get back at Willy, the kid sat in his car late at night while his parents were out and revved the engine *really loud.*

Willy waited until the kid went to bed and four hours later managed to unload a pound of popcorn into the muffler of the kid's car. We'll leave the result of this fun to your own imagination.

Willy denied everything when the parents and the kid came to see him. He generously offered to call the police. To date, a truce is in effect.

This next one is not really a new stunt, but it always seems to work and it's a pretty harmless practical joke. Thank Roger from Cincinnati for passing it along to us.

Your mark has a new car and brags about it incessantly. (It gets great gas mileage, of course.) If this gets tiresome, Roger says to help the mark out by adding a little gasoline to the car while he or she is not around. Get the mileage up to about 50 MPG.

Then, go the other way. Start to siphon out gasoline over a period of weeks, and get the rate down to about 15 MPG. You'll drive the mark nuts.

As I said, hardly new, but it always works and it's always a load of chuckles for all but the mark.

BABY-SITTER

Did you ever get trashed by a baby-sitter? Did one of these little bimbettes-in-training drink your booze, hump someone's boyfriend in your bed, ignore your kids, triple your phone bill, ruin your stereo, or snoop in your closets? Some of the above happened to Rev. Nasty, and this good holy man had a quick response.

Using a rented copy shop computer and Xerox machines, he produced a little flier that he posted on bulletin boards in supermarkets, laundromats, and community centers. The ad read something like this:

> BABY-SITTING IN YOUR HOME
> Single mother, 16, on nonviolent work release pro-
> gram needs work badly. Off drugs and alcohol for
> third and final time. Needs a chance. Also repre-
> sents modeling agency needing kiddie photos
> for commercial sales. Will work cheap.

The ad also included the name, address, and telephone number of the pilfering, drunken baby-sitter who had terrorized Reverend Nasty's family. A one-time dose of this exposure was quite effective, as Reverend Nasty heard from the usual small-town-gossip media.

BALLOON

Without getting into grand detail, suffice that a nasty old man had Brian from Denver fired from his part-time job solely to discourage Brian from being friends (nothing sexual) with the pusshead's daughter. He banished this daughter—his only child—to her grandparents for the week to keep the two apart.

To repay the man's insecurity, inhumanity, and lack of trust in both his daughter and Brian, our intrepid young hero managed to temporarily acquire three uninflated promotional balloons from a local fast-food restaurant.

Brian says the move was easy. He took the balloons to the home of his nemesis and quietly climbed onto the roof, where he moored all three after turning on the built-in silent inflator for each.

At dawn, early-rising neighbors saw three 20-foot-high Ronald McDonald balloons floating over their grumpy neighbor's house. Within an hour, local police were there too. Mr. Jerk received notice of a summary offense, only because the restaurant manager didn't wish to make waves with a trial.

Brian considered doing it again the following week to help change the manager's mind. Instead, he did something completely different, so as "not to become boring." That one is in the *Telephone* chapter.

By the way, could you possibly guess who called to tip the manager that the balloons were stolen and where they were? And can you guess that the call didn't come until dawn of that next day? Wrong; it wasn't Brian. The call came from out of town. Why, my goodness, it must have been . . .

Right.

BANKS

Do banks ever screw with you and yours? I get a lot of complaints from readers about banks. And if you do have a legit gripe, most of them pay no more attention to you than an elephant would to a flea climbing up its ass with intentions of sodomy.

Indeed, for the amount of interest my bank quoted me the last time I asked about a loan to buy a new pickup truck, they should have offered to shampoo my hair with caviar. I declined the loan.

I then paid attention to a suggestion from Piper Pub, this one with interest for two marks—one a bank and the other someone who owns a boat and/or fishes. Piper had a one-sided, running disagreement with his bank over some investments that they smugly told him to forget about. He also had a nastier disagreement with a man who owned a charter fishing boat.

"I went to a tackle shop to buy some special fishing equipment," Piper says. I bought several large metallic lures and took them home. Being careful not to leave fingerprints, I inscribed my mark's name and address at the marina on the lures. My next step was to attach some line and some weights. I took this over to the bank's night deposit box and tossed it all in. I wore gloves, of course."

Piper's mark probably had some explaining to do for some humorless federal types who were not about to swallow his fishy story hook, line, and sinker. Maybe we could call the cable TV series "Fishing for Greenbacks."

31

BAR BETS

Even if it's only for a free lemonade, bar bets are fun and even harmlessly amusing. My friend Houdini from New City, New York, offers you one. (There is another name for bar bets, of course, and we'll get to that in a moment.)

After several rounds, when the stories and challenges have reached a fairly low point on the intellectual scale, toss out the fact that you know how to light a match under water. Be aggressive, challenge your pals . . . it's bar bet time. Push the point; make it a personal challenge to them. Being assertive is the key to winning the only kind of bet there is—a sucker bet.

When the stakes are to your liking, get a glass of water and set it on the table. Then calmly reach under the table, strike a match directly below the glass, collect your winnings, and smile.

Houdini once told me that he noticed my address was a post office box, and he often wondered how I could live in something that small. I thought that was funny. He's OK. Houdini is also the only guy I know who can write his name backwards as quickly as I can do mine the normal way.

There is only one type of bet to make. An an old colleague, Herman Nethersnout, reminded me of that last year when he explained this arcane little bit of larceny to me. He had hatched it as a harmless bit of payback against a guy who was always betting silly amounts on silly things.

The guy had become an annoying friend.

Follow this dialogue along and see how Nethersnout made an easy ten bucks. We'll refer to Nethersnount as NS and his smartass friend as MRK, for Mark.

NS: Hey, I'll bet you ten bucks that you can't repeat and properly pronounce three words after I say them. Deal?

MRK: What kind of a jerk bet is that? Of course I can. You're on, fool.

NS: Platypus.

MRK: Platypus.

NS: Pterodactyl.

MRK: Pterodactyl.

NS: Wrong!

MRK: What? What the hell do you mean?

NS: You lost, pay up.

MRK: What the hell, I said pterodactyl!

NS: Yeah, you did, but the third word I said was the word *wrong*. Pay up, sucker.

Nethersnout claims to have used this one several times and to have won his ten bucks each time, but only with deserving people.

You don't like it? It was a great American journalist named Damon Runyon who wrote in the first half of this century that, "The race is not always to the swift, nor the battle to the strong, but that's the way to bet." Usually. . . although I wonder how Nethersnout and Runyon would have fared.

BARS

This works well if you're trapped by boring, obnoxious people while you're inside a bar, tavern, or other establishment that has security people (a.k.a. bouncers). Indeed, the less sophisticated the establishment, the better this stunt works.

Let's say you're being annoyed and badgered for a contribution from some religious fanatic while you're enjoying a couple of cold ones in a saloon. Now, this religious fundamentalist has a fiery cross up his ass and just won't leave you alone. Here's what you do.

You inform the bouncer that the religious lunatic is actually a homosexual who has made the most gross, obscene, and explicit propositions you've ever heard. You are shocked and want to call the police. The bouncer and the bartender don't want to see any police. Nor do they like gays.

Now, considering how much (1) these Bible-thumpers hate homosexuals, and (2) the usual macho-type bouncers fear gays, your mark is in for a real treat.

Am I picking on gays? Whooaaa, no way! I am picking on religious-nut fascists and the usual mental midget from the local high school who has pegged bar bouncer as his life's work after playing out his football eligibility with a minus GPA.

Sit back and enjoy, but be sure to maintain your indignant annoyance. You can use this ploy on virtually anyone who makes a major case out of bugging you in a bar.

WARNING: Please do *not* do this to people from the Salvation Army. They are good people—one of the few national charity outfits that really do care for poor folks. So give them money and don't pick on them. Also, they care for old drunks, so you might need them someday.

BIGOTS

Good God, there really are racial and religious bigots and snobs in this world, just like the villains in that wonderful film, the original *Caddyshack*. My old pal Seymour Butts was turned down for membership at a posh New York country club because his religion was not on the WASP-approved list of the board of directors. They even had the audacity to tell him to his face. His religion is . . . gasp . . . Jewish.

"George, between you and *Caddyshack*, I had some fun with them," Seymour told me. "I carefully and painlessly live-trapped four groundhogs and relocated them to the golf course. Soon, my furry friends had expanded the original eighteen-hole course to a thirty- or forty-holer. They also created five new groundhogs to help out in this holy mission for the pious bastards of the board."

Seymour then went out near the golf course at night and fired off a .22 rifle. After two nights, he made an anonymous phone call to the local game warden, claiming to be a club member, saying he'd heard that the board was hiring poachers to illegally shoot groundhogs.

"I shot a groundhog on my own place that afternoon, then planted it on a fairway. I saw the game warden's truck by the clubhouse a mile away, so I fired a couple of shots near the groundhog and left. I tipped the local newspaper about the story."

Seymour predicted that the local paper's do-gooder, animal-lover, anti-gun bias would color the story the way he wanted it, taking a cruelty-to-animals angle. He was right. The article also hinted at country club pressure placed on local political leaders to quiet the whole thing by stopping the game warden from looking into the issue.

Seymour said he plans to whack a stray dog or cat to leave for the warden to find, too, as he continues his holy crusade against religious intolerance.

Happy hunting and good shooting, amigo, whatever or whomever your payback targets may be.

BIKERS

News for the crew at Woodland Lounge, home of some of the most fun bikers Uncle Gerry and I ever partied with. Thanks to the Bronx Bomber, I learned how to pay back a rival biker who's done you or your bike awful.

"No details as to why I did this; it's too fresh. But simply apply some industrial-strength glue to the cylinders and/or other exposed working parts of his bike. It takes only two hours to immobilize the bike," Bronx says.

(See, Bonnie, I told you I'd get you into a book. It's taken a few years, but I did it.)

Ray Heffer told me about bug bombing the foundation of a house with some nasty bikers in it. He says to run a water hose into the foundation until you get about two feet of soak going. Then, dump a bunch of termites down the water hole and wish them "bon appetite."

Another Heffer special deals with those rubber turds you get from joke and novelty shops. When one of your biker marks gets hungry and orders a hot sausage or bologna sandwich (or something else that looks like an anal dumpling), you can make the substitution.

Bonnie once told me that she liked to serve them smeared with peanut butter and wrapped in toilet paper ... placed right in the roll. It never failed to gross out even the grossest of the gross bikers. I mean, knowing some of those guys, it could have been real. Think about it.

BOATS

Can you believe he's going to put out a roadkill calendar? I'm not sure when, but watch for it. That was the last word I had on the subject from Chris Scott. However, both he and Piper Pub came up with an interesting new use for roadkill. I feel that it shows some imagination and sensitivity, as well. But what does all of this roadkill stuff have to do with boats? Well, rest your oars for a moment and I'll tell you.

Someone invented soap on a rope, so how about roadkill on a boat? Wait, think about it. People like boats, so why can't roadkill enjoy boating? Don't be so damn stuffy and linear in your thinking.

Both Chris and Piper had boat owners do them in—one socially, the other professionally. As usual, no amount of decent dialogue resolved the situation. Both Chris and Piper used just about the same method of dealing with the tormentor, even though these Haydukers are a continent apart and don't know each other.

Each tied several samples of ripe, fresh, large-sized roadkill to the prop of his mark's boat with a sturdy line. The payoff? When the mark started his boat's engine, the propeller shaft quickly wrapped in the line, bringing the juicy, fresh roadkill into slice 'n dice contact with the prop's blades. The resultant colorfully graphic hors d'oeuvre made a major impact upon both marks' boat guests and other marina residents.

All I can think to add is, "good show, old chums."

Additionally, Piper suggested that you can stir up other boat owners against your mark if you pilfer their equipment and use it to equip your mark's boat. Before you do the actual transfer of nautical accessories, you can also drop subtle hints about the dishonesty of this mark.

It's fun when victims find their stolen goods on your mark's boat, especially in the social strata of the marina.

BOMBS

Technically, this idea really isn't a bomb, but that title surely does hype the thought. Grizzled wanted to raise some concern and visual excitement in a neighbor to whom he owed a minor payback. Grizzled's response was harmless and measured, but highly successful:

"I inserted a bunch of large primers for pistol ammunition into the splits and cracks of his outside firewood. I probably larded about a hundred of them in half a cord of wood," Grizzled said.

Not to worry, gentle reader, this is not dangerous. Primers explode loudly, but with far less force than a small firecracker. That is their effect—mystery. Everyone knows the firecracker boom, but few would recognize a pistol primer's crack. And again, there is little danger. They are available at better sporting goods shops everywhere.

However, as this section is about bombs, please pay attention. Willy Thornton has solved the problem of detonating bombs in and about your neighbor's property from a safe distance.

Without getting into technical detail here, Willy says you need to use an infrared sensor hooked to the fuse or triggering device, and you need to be a good shot with a Lasertag unit. Willy says if you understand that, you need no further instruction. I do, and I agree. See *Sources* or the sensors and most stores for the toy units.

BOOZE

Although it is ancient history that alcohol can be used for Haydukery purposes, the Razor has researched a far more subtle approach that he kindly shares with us. His instrument was a hypodermic syringe, and the ingredient was good old grain alcohol.

"I decided to test it on a couple of honeydew melons that I planned to serve to friends at a dinner in a couple of days. I shot those melons full of a goodly amount of grain.

"The guests ate the melons with no indication they suspected from taste or odor that anything had been added to the fruit. But, within ten minutes, several guests were noticeably intoxicated. All were louder than usual and acting very cheerful."

The Razor says the best alcohol additive is Everclear. It works well in booze-flavored candies, fruits, and the like. As the Razor told me, there is no limit here beyond your own imagination and however much hassle you want your mark to suffer.

Ray Heffer suggests another twist in which additives go into your mark's booze or other drinks. Ray says that many old-time bartenders keep a small bottle of croton oil behind the bar to deal with potentially nasty patrons. The stuff is a *very* powerful laxative.

Ray adds, "Unless your mark is standing next to the bathroom and has tearaway clothes, he or she just won't make it to the facility in time. Aren't the possibilities limitless?"

BUGS

Byron, our resident entomologist from California, comments that as most people are terrified of them, bees make wonderful companions for your mark. Actually, most people don't like bugs of any sort. But about bees, he's right on target . . . and you can be too. On the bright side, maybe your mark is allergic to bee-stings.

A particular business had not only ripped off a friend of Byron's, they'd gotten him into trouble with the police. He was threatened, arrested, and given a bad time through the insistence of the store.

Eventually, the police learned of the mistake, and myriad apologies were tendered. As his family was too proud and respectful to sue the police and too poor to sue the store owner, justice was left to Byron's friend.

Byron explains, "Bees are available from apiary supply houses as well as some farm supply shops. You can get two or three pounds of live bees for about three or four dollars.

"Bees come packed in little boxes with plugs. You remove the plugs and the bees slowly emerge into whatever environment they've been placed.

"There are more than enough bees in one pound to terrorize the hell out of most people," Byron adds. "Those little guys sure enjoyed playing around in that nasty store, just like miniature dive bombers."

Meanwhile, a vote comes in from Nor Razan for the preservation and use of cockroaches. Nor had a pal whose dishonorable real estate salesman placed him in a rental dump infested with that lovely pest, the cockroach. As you know, scientists say cockroaches are the only thing likely to survive a nuclear war, which may explain our recent voting patterns. But, I digress . . . .

Nor and his pal caught some cockroaches, then went to a pet supply house and got a pregnant female roach. They started delivering gift-wrapped packages of these ugly bugs to the real estate nasty at his home and office.

Their most fun parcel was sent to the guy c/o his boss' home one weekend. Did Mr. Salesman get the messy-age?

Nor says, "My buddy said they had a top exterminator at his complex Monday morning, and there were two follow-up calls from the rental sales guy."

BUMPER STICKERS

I'm always interested in hearing about new bumper sticker messages that you've created and/or used. Please let me know about your imaginative handiwork. Remember, you didn't actually place them anywhere, you just thought up the message. And anyway, it was all in good, clean fun.

My first selection of original bumper stickers to be honored came from the Mad Bomber of Steubenville and his magic imagination of how to decorate a mark's car, home, or whatever.

- LEGALIZE (NAME A DRUG) NOW!
- HONK IF YOU LIKE (NAME SOME BIZARRE SEX ACT)
- KILL ROCK 'n ROLL
- I'M NO VIRGIN. ASK YOUR MOTHER.
- SATAN IS MY GOD
- I ♥ LITTLE BOYS
- I EAT (NAME A COLOR OR ETHNIC GROUP) CHICKS (OR BOYS)

Other friends sent in photos or sketches of bumper stickers they had made for their marks' cars. Here are a few:

- EAT SHIT, WATERMELON LIPS
- WHITE TRASH & REDNECKS FUCKING = EARTHWORM SNAILS

Here is one of Dick Smegma's original designs, which, by the way, he also had reproduced as a business card, distributing a thousand in local airports, bars, store bulletin

45

boards, etc. Dick says if the mark has an unlisted telephone number it's even more fun. Here is his design:

DIAL A SHITHEAD . . . IT'S FUN !!
CALL (303) 555-6969 ASK FOR (MARK)
CALL 24 HRS.

As I indicated, please feel free to share your own original bumper sticker ideas. They—and you—could be infamous in the near future.

BURGLARS

Ellen from Cincinnati told me this story during a call-in radio show I did on WCKY. It seems that there was a truly nasty old witch, all of forty years old, who was the hated bitch of the neighborhood. She would have made Sam Kinison seem like a gentle holy icon. Ellen told me this broad had the personality of "sewer seepage," was a gossip, and was mean to little kids. Also, her dog took dumps in all of the neighborhood yards but her own.

I enjoyed Ellen's retaliatory response, an event with which she was in no way involved. Good thinking, Ellen!

"While the old biddy was away visiting her equally evil sister in Dayton, a burglar hit her place, stole the usual valuables, then trashed her house looking for other goodies.

"While I waited a week for the police to lose interest, I had plans for the mean lady. Using great care to avoid incrimination, I had a male friend make a 'thank you' telephone call to the old broad from the 'burglar,' noting that it was such fun to trash her place that he'd be back to do it again. He added that he hoped she'd be there so they could have fun in bed together, too," Ellen added.

She said she learned from neighbors that the police thought the woman was nuts when she called them, and that they eventually stopped their patrol past her place each night. Ellen had her friend call twice more, at four-week intervals, and lace his talk with sexual overtones.

Ahh, Cincinnati, I'll always have a warm memory of Cincinnati. Sigh.

CAMPERS

Calvin knew that his late fall camping trip was going to be bad when he saw the lady at the next site walking her dog, a pit bull wearing a cutesy plaid doggie sweater. The lady wasn't much better; her face looked like one of Walker Cooper's old catcher's mitts.

"I was right—the damn dog was a mean nuisance, barking at night, lunging and snarling at everyone," Calvin said.

Being a diplomatic guy, Calvin decided to make a peace offering. Recalling that there are two edible things most dogs cannot ignore—chocolate and Twinkies—he purchased chocolate-flavored laxative and a box of Twinkies from a nearby supermarket, combined the two into a doggie sandwich, then tossed them over to the pit bull while the mutt-faced lady was inside her camper frightening the spiders.

Calvin recalled with a chuckle or twelve, "Oh, life can be a real bitch when you're camping with a pit bull that can't control its bowels. Especially as I was leaving that very afternoon for a new site."

I wonder how the lady and her pit bull spent the day? Perhaps we could ask Mr. Whipple.

CAN OF SNAKES

Sure, we all know about that hoary old novelty shop item, the tall can labeled "candy" that, when opened, releases a scary, spring-loaded snake. It was kid's stuff. . . until Captain Video got hold of it.

Says the good Captain, "The twist is to put fine confetti —machine shop filings, grit, or some other fine substance— in a container on the head of the spring-loaded snake. That stuff is tough to clean out of a carpet, not to mention your mark's eyes or hair.

"Or, you could load the projectile with fecal matter, which will make a smelly mess on the carpet. It's also quite possible that the mark will have his head over the can when he or she opens it."

Captain Video has given us new meaning for the term "shitfaced."

Several other correspondents suggested pulling the same stunt with vomit, urine, dye, acid . . . and the list gets worse from there.

CHEMICALS

Some readers have written to ask me for the common household equivalents of various chemicals I have listed from time to time. Thanks to my major chemistry consultants, Rob M. and Bryan S., I am able to present that list now.

Chemical	Equivalent
acetic acid	vinegar
ammonium chloride	ammonia
carbon carbonate	chalk
carbon tetrachloride	cleaning fluid
calcium hypochloride	bleach powder
calcium oxide	lime
calcium sulfate	plaster of paris
carbonic acid	Alka-Seltzer
ethylene dichloride	dutch fluid
ferric oxide	iron rust
glucose	syrup
graphite	pencil lead
lead acetate	sugar of lead
lead tetroxide	red lead
magnesium silicate	talc
magnesium sulfate	epsom salts
phenol	Tylenol
potassium bicarbonate	tartar sauce
potassium nitrate	saltpeter

sodium dioxide	sand
sodium bicarbonate	baking soda
sodium carbonate	washing soda
sodium chloride	salt
sodium hydroxide	lye
sodium silicate	water glass
sodium sulfate	Glauber's salt
sodium thiosulfate	photographer's hypo
sulfuric acid	battery acid
zinc chloride	tinner's fluid

Richard, who tells me he's a covetous admirer of the legal profession, spreads the word on how to create a very potent, dry version of poison oak. His botanical friend swears by the process, and my own botanical consultant agreed that it is a practical methodology.

The nasty part of poison oak is soluble in alcohol. Use Everclear (or, if that's not available, the chemists tell me acetone will work too). Soak some very carefully gathered, pristine leaves from poison oak plants in the solvent of your choice.

Next, strain out the leaves and let the solvent evaporate (small aluminum pie pans work well). What you have left in the pans is *extremely* potent misery: poison oak powder.

Richard says only a truly nasty—or dedicated—person would apply this to any surface the mark would touch. You can combine the powder with a light oil as one delivery system. There are several other systems that come to mind.

Be careful; poison oak is nasty stuff.

Excalibur passes along the suggestion that you could spray a whole bunch of Mace or some similar product (e.g., CS gas) along the air conditioner intake of your mark's home or vehicle.

Speaking of such gas, suppose you can't or don't want to buy any. No problem, Grim Jack has a formula that will allow you to make it right in your own home.

Grim says to mix four ounces of glycerin and two ounces of powdered Sani-Flush toilet bowl cleaner into an empty can (small size) that may have contained wood stain or something similar. Be sure you've cleaned the can with solvent and dried it first, please.

Heat the mixture and leave . . . once it starts boiling and steaming, everyone within eye or nose range is in trouble. Obviously, you need to cover it to use later as a projectile, or you need to handle the boiling stage in the mark's environment.

That's Grim Jack; never a dry eye in the house when he's done.

COMPUTER

Excalibur, formerly a military policeman, is professionally familiar with stun guns, the electronic age's version of a blackjack. They put out about forty thousand volts of kickass power that overrides the target's voluntary nervous system.

Purely as a hypothetical question, Excalibur wants to know what happens to the IC chips in a computer terminal when it gets hit by a stun gun, or about eight thousand times its maximum voltage? You have an expensive pile of burned-out parts, is his response. He says it takes about ten seconds of juice to destroy a home computer.

"Don't take my word for it," he says. "Buy one of those four-dollar calculators at Radio Shack and try it out with a stun gun. Anything with a microprocessor in it is a potential victim."

I believed him, but I wanted to try it anyway. I fried a small calculator. This device will also work on stereos, radios, and TV sets. Excalibur said some of his pals used their stun guns to wreck the radios of pimps and other street punks (both in their cars and on their persons).

That's heavy ZAP, friends.

CONDOMS

Just when we thought we'd explored every useful application of a condom, Billy Buttreamer presents yet another. His idea is to bring some hidden and hostile anxieties out of someone's closet. His method is very simple.

According to Billy, there is a condom on the market known as "Man-to-Man," intended for gay couples. Billy had a really sicko mark whose major claim to anything was his low-mentality posturing about his virile, macho image. When this jerk did some truly bad Robert Chambers-type things to a lady, Billy helped out with the aftermath.

He sent a pack of the Man-to-Man condoms to the mark's boss (it could also go to a close friend, a biker, or whomever) along with a short note on the mark's personal stationery, which had been pilfered by the lady whose health—and, I guess, honor—was in question.

The message from the mark was an honest, explicit love note to the boss filled with pious hoo-hoo about safe sex and all that. It concluded with a proposition to "just talk things over" and a brief, lustful outburst about how the mark wanted to . . . well, I suspect you've put this together.

If the message recipient is obviously straight, the response is predictable. If the message recipient is not straight, the response ought to be a real shock to the mark. Either way, Billy wins. The mark does not.

Billy added that he leaked rumor of this odd liaison to the appropriate gossips of all three sexual persuasions.

CONTESTS

Even if you've never won anything, you are about to, and this stunt will explain how. You can use this to get vengeance on a human or institutional mark. It revolves around contests in which a store or some other institution provides an entry box for customers to deposit slips of paper with their names, addresses, and telephone numbers, in hopes of winning prizes.

Relieve that entry box of twenty or thirty entry forms. Then call all of those people and tell each one that he or she has won the Big Prize. To make it sound official, you say they must bring positive ID and be at the main office at some specific time/date. Naturally, you need to know the name of the boss/mark to whom they'll report.

Come that day and time, you will have a lot of very confused, frustrated, and angry ex-customers in a confrontation with Mr./Ms. Boss/Mark. This impacts either the institution or the person—your choice.

This stunt is a composite effort featuring bits and suggestions from such folks as Franz Fisher, the Renegade, Ivan Gemuetlichkeit, and the Gunslinger.

As a variation, you can also pick your specific mark and have him or her "win" a major prize from some secondary mark. The details work the same way, of course.

COSMETICS

According to Master Timothy J., you can even use cosmetics as an improvised additive to have fun with other items. For example, he says to buy six or seven cans of Arid Extra-Dry spray and one closet-door-sized full-length mirror.

Spray two cans of Arid per door, until the mirror is solid white. Let it dry for twenty-four hours, then scrape off the residue. Do the same until all of your Arid is gone. You now have what Master Timothy J. calls "great awful magic powder."

According to this young alchemist, one ounce of powder per automobile gasoline tank will mess up an engine. A single teaspoon will obliterate a ten-gallon fish tank and its denizens.

There are probably other uses for this by-product. And who says that America's young minds are not being productive anymore?!!

Further proof comes from this little run-through of helpful hints from Rev. Willy's cosmetic supply cabinet.

• Put condoms on the cucumbers or bananas in your mark's refrigerator.

• If you don't like your mark's brand of mouthwash, please substitute one of your own choosing. One of Rev. Willy's favorites is a combination of urine and blue food coloring.

• Or, perhaps the mark's shampoo or conditioner offends you. A good substitute is fresh tree sap—alone or with food coloring.

• Does your mark enjoy snacking while attending to

his/her toilet routine? If the snack of choice is nachos, you might want to share (i.e., spread some Cheese Whiz on light bulbs, in shower fixtures, on the toilet seat, and on radiators, furnaces, and furnace filters).

And so it goes in the magic coverup world of cosmetics. It's almost enough to make you think next time you . . . .

COURTS

The Renegade's best friend had been a police officer before resigning over poor pay to become a private investigator. This friend knows many ways to use our court system to sodomize deserving marks. In the interest of sharing useful knowledge, I offer the following examples from the Renegade's PI pal.

Posing as your mark, appear before the Clerk of Courts at your local courthouse and file divorce papers against "your" spouse. The filing fee is usually about $10 to $15. If the papers are properly completed and you look the part, the officials rarely ask for identification. Request that a sheriff's deputy serve the papers. This will probably cost you another ten spot, but it's well worth it. May I suggest that you time this action around some family event in the mark's life (e.g., anniversary, family reunion).

Let's play Subpoena the Witness. The first step is to check the docket with the court administrator's office and locate a fun-sounding civil case. Learn who the attorney is for one of the parties. Now, go to the Clerk of Courts office and identify yourself as an assistant to that attorney you researched. Inform the clerk that your boss needs to have a witness subpoena served on the mark's name.

Because this paper is a court order, the mark will have to show up. At the very least, your mark will have to hassle a lot of telephone calls to find out what's happening. But, if you're really lucky, the schmuck will go to court and sit for several hours, just waiting.

Court and courthouse stuff really can be fun if you make the rules and laws work for you, according to the Renegade.

CREDIT CARDS

To make all of this happen, Tommie Titmouse says you'll need the mark's Social Security number (which is fairly easy to obtain) and some additional personal history. You can make up the rest of the "facts" you need to answer questions on the credit card applications you are filling out and applying for in the name of your mark.

Go for the fancy credit cards with high annual fees. Go for the big ones that have snooty lawyers lacking in humor. Go for them all—everyone needs several dozen credit cards. You're helping your mark to realize that.

And, as a modest side benefit, maybe all of the confusion and bureaucracy created by myriad inquiries as the applications are being processed and investigated will damage the mark's credit rating for real.

Speaking of which, as long as you've gone to these lengths to impersonate the mark, why not try to get a copy of his or her credit rating? It's not that tough once you have the basic identification plus some cleverly created, legal-looking documents. Now *that* would be a powerful weapon in your war against your mark.

CYA

For the uninitiated, CYA refers to Cover Your Ass, or protecting yourself by establishing a good cover, be it a story, identity, alibi, or whatever. Houdini first suggested that I include some sort of "Rules for Good Cover," and I agreed. I talked with a couple of friends from the old days for their suggestions. So, from Houdini and others, here are the CYA rules.

First, get good books on the topic—build a reference library for solid, professional instruction in basic tradecraft. May I suggest *Undercover Operations*, by Kingdon Peter Anderson; *Undercover Work*, by Burt Rapp; *Spygame*, by Scott French and Lee Lapin; and *Making Spies*, by H.H.A Cooper and Lawrence Redlinger (all available from Paladin Press). Also, may I recommend Raymond Palmer's fine book, *The Making of a Spy* (published by Crescent Books, a division of Crown Publishers). Those are your best basic reference texts.

Here are a few simple rules to start you off until you can learn more from the professional references I've suggested.

1. The very best cover is always a simple extension of the truth.

2. Never volunteer information you are not asked for. If you explain little details when no one asked for them, people will either become very bored or very suspicious. If you're Hayduking, you cannot afford the latter.

3. Try to keep all cover and all cover stories as simple

and as close to reality as possible. If your cover must, by necessity, be elaborate, be certain that you have adequate documentation to back you up. However, never produce this documentation unless asked to . . . remember Rule 2.

4. The more elaborate your cover and the resultant documentation becomes, the more certain you must be that you have dealt with all details and options for problems before you go operational.

5. When under cover, it is vital that you stay in character at all times. More undercover people have been burned because they slipped out of character than for any other reason.

Ahhh, ain't tradecraft grand fun?

DEATH

While someone called death life's last practical joke, the Renegade and his PI pal make death more useful, literally making a practical joke of death. This stunt is a biggie and it will work. I can just hear some reader asking, "Now, how would he know that?" Trust me, it works.

We're going to bureaucratically kill your mark. The first step is to locate, then confiscate for your own use later —or destroy—his or her major ID cards (e.g., birth certificate, driver's license, state identification card, voter registration card, passport, Social Security card, employee ID card, etc.) Destroy or confiscate as many and as much as you can.

The next step is to obtain a death certificate; these forms vary from state to state. Fill it in with your mark's name, of course. Then, in accordance with your state law, file it at the courthouse in the county in which your mark was born. (In most states you must file it in the county of birth.)

Now you can run his or her obituary in every news medium available to you. If the media people check at the courthouse, they'll find a properly filed death certificate. The obits will run, and the mark is officially dead. Now, do you see why you nicked and destroyed all of the mark's identification? This makes it mighty, mighty tough to prove that he or she is who he or she claims to be.

If all goes well, when the mark tries to straighten all of this out, he or she will encounter suspicious clerks who think that the person in question is dead and that somebody else is now trying to pull a fast one. Perhaps you could step up the ante by making a phone call to the local law enforcement people about some suspicious person trying to get false ID and "start a new life." Hint at drugs or satanism.

You can also file a petition of probate about a week after the death certificate. This involves your mark's will and estate. This step will be of major interest to insurance company investigators and other quasi-legal types searching out fraud.

Death has many ways of inflicting, doesn't it?

DOGS

One of modern life's mysteries is why the neighbor's well-fed dogs still must root through your garbage bags, scattering trash for yards. Then you—not the neighbor or the dogs—pick up the mess.

Never mind that. My friends Sue, Karen, Shaun, and Chris asked me about a nasty little rat dog that terrorized their neatly bagged garbage while ignoring the slop piles of its owner. A bit of research showed that he sprayed his own parcels with an odor that repelled dogs.

It was a simple matter to switch formulae. We sprayed dog-away repellent on the good folks' bags and all sorts of food-smelling goodies on the owner's bags. At night I eased into the area and poured bacon and hamburger grease on the mark's garbage bags. I also circled my friend's bag area with lion skat from the local zoo.

Well, it wasn't too tough for the little rat dog to make some basic choices here. The good guys' garbage was shunned and the dog owner's bags were torn and their contents scattered about the yard. At the end of a month, the mark's nasty little dog was restricted to the house, and nobody's garbage was ever scattered again. Isn't that a nice story? And, it's true. I included it here to prove once more that Haydukery can be used for very uplifting and positive change.

DRUGS

Once upon a time, Evil Eddie loaned his car to a friend for a quiet date. The kid got drunk and wrecked the car to the amount of about eight hundred dollars. He was very sorry, but offered no cash to help pay for the damage. Eddie paid the repair bill himself and let his personal payback rest for a few months.

Because this mark had suspicious, overbearing parents, most of Eddie's payback was fairly easy and quite effective. Here are but a few of his drug-related paybacks:

• Evil Eddie had an older friend call the mark's mother and—sounding very concerned—tell her that the pot her son had bought last week was contaminated with Agent Orange. He hung up. She and the old man braced the kid for an hour over that one, then grounded him.

• Using a quick-copy service PC, Evil Eddie designed and printed business cards for the mark offering products to get high legally. He used the kid's home address and phone number. The cards were posted on school bulletin boards and in teen hangouts. Screaming his innocence, the mark was grounded for two weeks after police brought the cards to the house.

• Evil Eddie swiped a doctor's prescription pad from a clinic and made several really obvious forgeries for drugs using his mark's name. This one worked wonders too, resulting in more groundings, a thicker police file, and warnings about arrest. The kicker was that the mark never figured out or even considered how these things were happening. Not only did he tell Evil Eddie everything that was going wrong, he even asked his advice about what to do. Eddie was very understanding and asked a few questions of his own as he comforted his friend.

"Why did I ask questions? Well, I wasn't done with him yet," Evil Eddie explained. "I thought I might pick up on something further I could do to reclaim something."

My old pal, the Rubber Fox from Nashville, told me he once knew a man who really had a major payback due on a local businessman who'd stiffed him on a loan. Then he read in the newspaper that a local druggie had died of an overdose.

Using the businessman/mark's name and giving out his unlisted telephone number, Fox's pal called the dead guy's family to inquire if the deceased had left any of his drugs around, and if so, would they sell them to him.

He did this four more times when drug-related deaths were reported. After the third call, the police were in contact with the mark.

The neat thing about using drugs as a payback is the current hysteria. I mean, absolute, uninformed, media-frothed hysteria over drugs is sweeping poor, paranoid America. Our elected things, those bastard politicians, are taking full advantage to wrap themselves in yet another flag-waving issue. I spoke with one politico who was so dumb about drugs he thought antacid was an insect hallucinogen.

If, indeed, the drug cartel has America by the nose, you can use your heads, friends, to have your mark by the balls. I realize that was a sexist analogy, but, well . . . never mind.

DRUNKS

There is much that can be said for, about, and against drunks. For example, when a drunk pleads that he'll quit, he or she usually means it until the next drink is poured. In 1989 when John Tower was being piously gang-raped by his former colleagues of the U.S. Senate who were getting back at him for being a prick for twenty-four years, he sadly claimed he would quit drinking. Usually, this plea is heard by disgusted spouses from their respective souses who are facedown on the bedroom or bathroom floor.

Jimmy Breslin wrote *Table Money*, a very readable book with a central theme being the drunken sociography of its characters. And it's real because the people are real. We know them; we are them.

Giving up drink is easy; like W.C. Fields, I have done it hundreds of times. But, I owe credit for the greatest rating scale for drunkenness to a very good friend named David Hazinski, an ethical man who quit NBC News for strong ethical purposes and personal reasons. I have shared numerous lemonades with David over the years and have witnessed his scale of drunkenness in action (or perhaps inaction would be the better word). Perhaps it will help you. It didn't help John Tower.

When you or someone you know drinks copious amounts of booze, the imbiber will pass through the following stages, according to Professor Hazinski:

1. Witty, charming, clever, and polite.
2. Rich, powerful, and sexy.

3. Benevolent, clairvoyant, and sophisticated.

4. Even sexier and possessing a secret past.

5. Ahh, fuck dinner.

6. Patriotic—let's kill ragheads.

7. Sloppy-witty, semi-charming, pseudo-sexy.

8. Invisible.

9. Knee-walking.

10. Bulletproof.

As Ms. Nomore said to Mr. Onemore, she was tired of sitting around every night watching him perform that alcoholic magic trick of first swelling his liver to the shape of the Goodyear Blimp, then rotting it down to a dried prune. But I digress into sermon. Please excuse me, it must have been that last drink.

The Bronx Bomber dislikes disruptive, noisy, and obnoxious drunks. He described his cure as follows.

"I dislike these asshole drunken amateurs who impersonate lampshades. How does coarse sea salt sound for an anecdote? It is commercially available, and here is how you use it.

"Wait until you're up against an impossible drunk, the one who is guzzling from the bottle, peeing on the floor, grabbing people's parts, kissing corpses, and so on. Mix some of the sea salt into the mark's drink.

"Work up the dose rate as the souse gets more so. Soon, the mark will retch violently in the middle of whatever and wherever ... BARRROOOOMWOOOOSSSHHHH ...."

I've seen it work. One guy barfed so hard his shoes came out of his mouth near the end of the flood. Yeah, I love the Bomber's idea, but I caution you to pick the place or the host or hostess carefully, as they are not likely to be amused by the mark's action. Of course, the host and hostess could be mark II in a related scenario.

EARTH FIRST!

The editorial credo of my books is offbeat humor and counterculture theater designed to irritate the politically powerful—but morally pissant—establishment. There is some seriousness, of course, and in that regard, I am most sincere in my blessing and full support of the principles and principals for which Earth First! fights.

This is one section of the book where I am absolutely serious, with no tongue-in-cheek or hidden gotcha 'n guffaw. I have read and heard establishment enemies threaten EF! and its people with everything from total debt to prison to death.

Their more cultural critics call them "tree-huggers and granola crunching, nature-loving anarchists who don't care about the 'real' issues." The well-dressed gestapo from the Reagan/Bush Directorate of Injustice call EF! "a clandestine cult of subversive terrorists bent on destroying our industrial society and the American way of life."

Others, who are less greedy—and therefore more rational—see Earth First! as a last line of defense for our poor old battered planet, which is being devoured by the voracious pests to whom it is the unwilling host. Human beings are those pests.

Earth First! is fighting the land rapists who plunder under the euphemism of "developer," all the while destroying our planet, and eventually, all forms of life on it—us included. These land rapists are the same greedy bastards who've burned through the ozone layer and murdered the rain forests. And, wake up, gentle reader, these are not just environmental issues. They are very real attacks on the world in which we all must live. These attacks must be stopped, because they are killing our world for greed.

Obviously, the governments of the world won't stop these land rapists because those same governments—the United States included—are owned by the men who are destroying the world. If you really think you elect your government and that we are free, WAKE THE HELL UP! We don't own our country or our destiny anymore. They were taken away from us by that very same wealthy, powerful industrial oligarchy that rules through political puppets. To my knowledge, Earth First! is the only organized group doing anything to stop this oligarchy's greedy exploitation of our world. If you want to help save whatever is left for us, please support the Earth First! movement (Earth First! P.O. Box 210, Canyon, California 94516).

EGGS

It's no eggsaggeration that here is a good eggsample of egging on your mark and his ride. Beanie the Bandit and some friends had a run-in with a nasty guy and his girlfriend. These dishonest slugs had bilked Beanie out of some equipment and told him to get lost when he asked for either payment or return.

After the usual nice-guy attempts to rectify the matter, Beanie decided to shell the mark and his girlfriend, and here is how he did it.

"A friend called Mr. Mark, and, posing as a bar owner, told him that his girlfriend was in 'his' bar, drunk and causing trouble. My pal told Mr. Mark that he'd better come and get the lady or the police would be called," Beanie said, adding that the lady was a lush, anyway.

When the mark left the house and took off in his car for the bar, Beanie and his pals tossed buckets of raw goose eggs at his car from ambush points set up along the route. Some went into the car through the open windows. The guy almost wrecked. In a panic, he returned home.

"My friend called again and told the mark that his lady had gone to a bar down on the street *after* breaking his bar's front window with a thrown chair," Beanie related.

The mark was told that he had ten minutes to collect the drunken broad and pay the damages in cash, or the cops would be there in eleven minutes.

"The dumbshit started to leave again. This time we ambushed him as he pulled out of his driveway and again at the stop sign at the end of his block. We also drove after him in a pickup truck with two guys in the back heaving more eggs at him."

When Beanie's boys got close to the downtown area, they peeled off and drove away. Their next call was to the police to report that an angry madman was careening around town in an egg-splattered 1988 Ford Fairlane and give them the license number.

The man was arrested and taken to jail, then to court. His girlfriend? Oh, she was at the movie theater with another lady that evening and didn't know about any of this until he called their place around 2:00 A.M. to get her to come downtown and bail him out of jail.

According to Beanie, the yolk was finally on the mark, who also had to shell out some bread for a hefty fine for various offenses.

FARTS

To bring you up to date, I instituted a fart/belch poll several books ago to note the favor/disfavor trend among readers toward these humorous bodily functions. The poll is an ongoing research effort and is being coordinated by the prestigious Anderson Institute of Gastronomical Physics at Escobar University in Hooyek, Yugoslavia.

As of this writing, the poll is showing a wide margin in favor of those who enjoy the humor of gas passing and blowing (i.e., farting and belching). Of the results tabulated to date, 68 percent strongly favor the humor and usefulness of farting and belching, while 14 percent did not. Thirteen percent didn't care one way or the other, and the remaining 5 percent of respondents didn't understand.

With that in mind, I recall an amusing story that Alex was telling us in Mexico about being abused by the stench of rude cigarette smokers who persisted in blowing their odorous debris in her direction. She asked for help.

Quick to help a friend, Renee told how her daughter, a chip off the shapely young blockess, handled rude smokers using her own special talent. Renee explained, "My sweet, darling daughter soon tires of asking nicely, then she pointedly says that the smoke bothers her. When the bastard ignores her, she walks over, points her lovely derriere directly into the smoker's face and from a range of about 4 inches blasts out a fart that would register 7 on the Richter scale."

Renee said that one such incident sent the mark-smoker

sprawling off his chair. In another bombastic response, daughter's flatus attack not only blew the cigarette out of the man's mouth, it also toppled his chair with him on it.

"However, my daughter is multitalented," Renee added sweetly. "It was actually her belching that got her pledged to her sorority in college."

All of which brings out the philosopher in me—a disgusting side effect of growing older, I fear. But, you know, the more I think of such things I am convinced that the world will not end with a major, loud BANG, despite dire predictions by myriad moral malcontents. No, our world will come to its demise merely with the sound of wind breaking. And even *that* may be a dubious privilege.

FISH

Uncle Chris and some of his co-workers needed to come up with a minor annoyance to repay a nasty, uncivilized owner of an outdoor restaurant. There was a vacant field right next to the restaurant's outdoor patio and service area. And, as Uncle Chris and friends worked for an environmental engineering company and had been cleaning up a large fishkill from a nearby river, they had access to a lot of dead fish.

"Thus, the all-American game of carpball was born," Uncle Chris explained. "It's played just like stickball, only we used a Wiffleball bat and a rolled-up fish for a ball. Hitting one on the restaurant lawn was a single. If your batted fish landed on someone's table, it was a double. If you hit the restaurant building, you got a triple; and if your batted fish landed on the roof, it was a homer."

Play-by-play noted that it was not a pitcher's game; there were lots and lots of hits.

The game didn't last long. It was called on account of the police, who were notified by the restaurant guy. The police were quite amused (nobody liked the restaurant guy), but also quite firm about not harassing the restaurant guy. The restaurant patrons' reactions varied between outrage and outright hilarity. Some wanted to join the game. Uncle Chris and friends were just being good sportsmen. The fish? What did they care, they were already dead.

And what do you say to start a game of Carpball just before dinner? Why, "Batter up," of course.

FOOD

Food has become a very fashionable accessory for the new decade—a definite part of the lives of the beautiful, upscale people who matter. That's why you're probably puzzled to read about it here. You're reading it largely because of Grim Jack.

Grim Jack should get your kudos for his happy helpings to the menu for this section. He has some clever ideas for some ersatz food for your mark's menu. Grim, it's all yours . . . what are today's blew palate specials?

• Homemade Expectorant: If someone is always mooching or stealing your food, feed them something spitful instead of spiteful. Combine a handful of finely chopped lawn grass with mustard. On bread, it will look just like mustard relish. The kicker? The human digestive system can't process grass. Unless your mark is descended from bovines, his tummy processes are in trouble. Where does the term "expectorant" come into this? Ever watch a dog or cat perform after it's eaten grass? Yup, that's right. Don't let the mark get any on you.

• Pasty Ice Cream: So, your mark loves ice cream. Try mixing one or two tubes of mint-flavored toothpaste with a half gallon of vanilla or mint ice cream. This mixes better if the ice cream is slightly soft; it can all be hardened later. The kicker? Toothpaste is also indigestible—ask your pharmacist, doctor, or dentist . . . or George Bush, for crissakes!

By now, your mark will be all filled up . . . well, sort of.

FUNERALS

You know you're really getting ancient when you start attending more funeral services for friends than divorce parties or, occasionally, weddings. On the other hand, sometimes funerals are excellent places for Haydukery.

Why should a hired theologian have a monopoly on the mourners' grief? Someday you may just find yourself in a funeral situation where Hayduking would be an appropriate way for you to assist in augmenting the grief of those who really deserve it.

With a hearty "thank you" to such folks as Ivo Rinon, Clem Carpball, and Ed Bluestone, all of whom contributed mightily from their vast knowledge of funeral home humor, I have compiled the following list of things you can do at a funeral service.

• Tell the widow that the deceased's last wish was that she give you a warm yogurt enema or perform oral sex upon you at, or after, the service.

• Pull out the deceased's tongue and use it to lick stamps for your picture post cards.

• Insert a lighted cigar in the deceased's mouth and set a mug of beer on his chest or in his hand . . . or a deck of fanned cards.

• Ask the family how they plan to pay off all of the gambling or drug debts run up by the deceased.

• Tell the family that you have to leave for vacation so they should skip the sermons and eulogies—the boring stuff —and just get to the reading of the will.

• Tell other mourners that the deceased told everyone else how bitterly he/she hated that person. Ask each to leave the service.

• If there is soft chamber music, accompany it with a jew's-harp or kazoo.

• Ask the family to have someone take a photo of you clowning around with the deceased "for old time's sake."

• Arrange to slip inflated Whoopee cushions under the seats of the family and the holy man.

• As the processional convoy heads for the cemetery, pass other mourners' cars, weave in and out, then get behind the hearse and tailgate it, honking your car's horn.

That will do for a starter kit. I'm sure you can use your own fertile imagination to add twists and stunts of your own. But remember, don't get too serious about all of this. Francois Marie Aroulet, who used the pen name Voltaire, wrote about three hundred years ago that "Animals have these advantages over man: they have no theologians to instruct them, their funerals cost nothing, and no one starts lawsuits over their wills."

FURNACE

It's tough to imagine an easygoing nice guy like Ray Heffer getting angry. Yet, there was one time, he told me, when a store was so nasty to him that even he got angry. Not only did they charge him with theft, they said he'd done it in the past. Ray hadn't been in the store in months. It took him a lot of hassle and a few bucks worth of lawyer to prove his point and disprove theirs.

That's when he decided to collect his own punitive damages in his own way.

"The store sold home improvement stuff, so I had my friend go to the furnace filter department. Now, as you know, these things aren't sealed in plastic, they're right out in the open air.

"My pal squirted various scented materials on many of the filters, varying from fox urine to skunk scent—even insecticides like SEVIN or Dursban. I had thought of some vomit-inducing spray, but we'll hold on that for awhile.

"A chemist told me the scents would be absorbed and go unnoticed until the filters were in use, with air blowing though them. From the reports I got from a source inside the store, it was a real delight when angry customers started showing up at the manager's office with these foul filters," Ray explained.

As a footnote to his revenge, Ray added that he'd located a neat little squirter. It's called a Solder Sucker, and it's a rubber ball-type syringe with a narrow Teflon tip at the end—kind of like a miniature turkey baster. It squirts a good, strong stream a fair distance, Ray reports.

See, Ray's a nice, helpful guy. Me? My advice to Ray would have been to shove a cattle prod up the store manager's ass and put his genitals on a trickle charge. But, that's why I'm me and Ray isn't. He's nice.

GIFTS

One of our society's pressing problems is what sort of gift to get for that special person who has everything. That's why I'm happy to have a friend like Biggus Piraphicus, a friendly Texan with a perfect gift suggestion for everyone in need of such personal advice.

Here is a little peek into Biggus's gift list of perfect presents for your deserving mark.

• Send violets or other purple flowers to a superstitious mark who also happens to be Brazilian. Purple is their death color. In a similar sense, send white to a Chinese mark. To a Mexican mark, yellow flowers are a symbol of death.

• Give the gift of cutlery to any old-line, old-time European sophisticate. In their lexicon of conduct, a knife wounds a friendship.

• Know a French person whom you hate? (That wouldn't be hard to find.) Nonetheless, have your favorite FTD florist—or Merlin Olson—deliver yellow flowers or chrysanthemums. Yellow flowers mean infidelity, and mums are only for funerals in France.

• If your mark is a married Arabic woman, you can give her a fifth of your least favorite rotgut whiskey. This could be considered a double—maybe even a triple—whammy if the booze is truly offensive in its lack of quality.

Which reminds me of the time way back in early '89 when I ran a series of small ads in a never-mind-where publication offering autographed copies of Salmon

Rushdie's *The Satanic Verses* at cut-rate prices. The "advertiser" listed was a very deserving mark whose unlisted home telephone number was included in the advertisement. The publication reached many folks of the Islamic faith.

GOD

Whoever said that God has no sense of humor obviously doesn't know Her. As evidence of God's sense of humor, I present the following story that the Establishment Gestapo can blame on nobody but....

Lightning killed New England Electric CEO Samuel Huntington while he was hiking in the Colorado Rockies. He had just addressed an energy forum in Aspen about the marvels of pollution-causing energy.

There have to be other such ironies out there....

HOMOPHOBIA

If you have a major case of homophobia, get over that redneck hang-up right now. Use this asinine fear to real advantage against some real asshole (pun intended). Here is a hilarious stunt as performed by Carla Savage, a truly class lady all the way.

Not too long ago, she had a business associate who needed to be knocked down a few pegs because of some grief he was causing little people who couldn't afford to fight him in court.

Carla has a good male friend who loves to wear pretty dresses on days other than Halloween; the guy is dazzlingly gay, as opposed to being a breeder. Her friend wanted to help her truly demolish the business sleaze.

At a major social event in front of dozens of people, Carla's friend—in a lovely dress and all made up in a travesty of gaydom—rushed up to the businessman and his astonished wife (who, by the way, looked more like Victor McLaglen than the husband did). The gay grabbed the man in an embrace and kissed him square on the lips. He held him solidly, as this gay guy (according to Carla) is quite strong, and the business jerk is not.

Then, shrilling for all to hear while pointing theatrically at the wife, the queen screamed, "What is *she* doing here, darling? You never told me you had a cover.

"Let's ditch the bitch and have some fun, lover," he laughed, taking the stunned businessman by the arm. "You didn't call the other night. What's the matter, still a bit tender down there?"

Eventually, order was restored, but then, this bastardly businessman had gained a new reputation as a result of the incident. Rumors began and continued for months.

HOSTAGE

This is an intriguing idea because it's been done before, but usually not well. Taking a mark hostage and doing fun things has contemporary genesis in the film *Animal House*; it surfaces in the porno classic, *Behind the Green Door*, and in historic features and fiction forever.

It still is an intriguing idea, as both Brian Roe and Hastings Pajawonk have outlined. In composite, they suggest you invite your mark to some social event in which stimulants abound. Then, while the mark is still aware, you stage a scuffle and kidnapping, during which the mark is blindfolded, gagged, and kidnapped. Make a lot of noise and protest, make it sound as if you're fighting to rescue the mark.

This part of the scenario is vitally important. It must appear to be real . . . very real. And it must appear that you are not involved in the stunt, other than trying to save the mark. When asked later, you know nothing beyond the scuffle and seeing "someone" leave with the mark. Get your cover story straight before you start.

Next, the mark is stripped of all clothing as he or she is driven to a secondary mark's home location (e.g., school official, religious leader, boyfriend or girlfriend, parents, the other parents, police chief, grandparents, whomever).

Upon arrival, the blindfolded, gagged mark is spread-eagled and tied to sturdy stakes that have been driven into the ground. At this point, depending upon the time and the amount of attention you've gained, you can either split or attract the attention of the secondary marks by the usual means.

Brian suggests that you videotape the entire adventure, being careful to keep the identities of the Haydukers secure. Still photos could also be taken.

HOUSES

Bryan was really upset with some neighbors who saved a few bucks by hiring el cheapo scab labor of the non-greencard variety to do very extensive remodeling on their home. The guys began work at 11 P.M. and worked until 4 A.M., creating an orchestrated cacophony of hammers, power saws, air guns, and cursing, plus several boom boxes blasting very high-volume conflicts of rock and salsa.

"I was a nice neighbor and tried every reasonable, rational way I could on behalf of the rest of us whose sleep was being totally ruined. Nowhere, that's where I got, nowhere," Bryan said.

In desperation, he plotted payback. Sardines and tuna joined his family menu big time. He saved the oil. He boiled some cruddy chickens for soup and saved the fat that floated up. He got old cooking oil from friends. Then, he began to help decorate the remodeling job while the owners and their mental-midget helpers were away.

"I poured some of the slop into their light fixtures to gum up things. I rubbed it into any bare wood surface that would absorb it. This was early spring . . . I knew what would happen in the heat of summer."

Bryan also rubbed old mayonnaise under the lips of stair steps. He splashed jars of old beer urine that he had been fermenting for weeks onto the stucco around the frame.

Bryan adds, "My only regret is that due to a new job I had taken, we moved before summer and missed the full impact of this special decorative charm I'd added to their new home."

But, thanks to other neighbors, Bryan was informed that every single little additive he put into the remodeling job came out in full bloom with the summer heat.

JOKES

An American writer named Max Eastman observed that repartee was a duel fought with the points of jokes. Dick Smegma has sharpened the blade quite a bit. He suggests you publish a joke book about your mark.

"It's easy, especially with the new laser printers or the ones now available in copy shops. You get a really raunchy, foul book of dirty insult jokes. You pick out the worst ones and 'write' your own joke book, substituting the mark's name for that of the object of each joke." For example:

"Hey, what happens when acid is thrown in MARK's face?"

"His/her looks are improved."

Or,

"MARK is so stupid that when he/she tried to rob a bank, she/he tied up the safe and blew up the guard."

Or,

"What happened to MARK when he/she got sent to prison?"

"The brothers used his ass like the Holland Tunnel."

I think you get the idea, as I'm sure Dick knew you would. Well, happy publishing to you, your imagination, and your mark. And remember, it's all in fun . . . for entertainment purposes only.

LANDLORD

This landlord was so bad he would be charged with littering at a crack house. That was the kind of person running an apartment complex in Atlanta, where he gouged rent, was a cruel racist without cause, and cheated everyone. My friend Neal suggested a clever way to add some perspective to this jerk's life.

"Through a friend I got hold of a plain rental van. We made up a large, professionally done sign for both sides of the van."

That sign read:

AIDS MOBILE TESTING UNIT
PUBLIC HOUSING DIVISION

"We parked the van in the street, right across from the parking lot of this asswipe's apartment building," Neal said. "We were directly across from his rental office."

There was a great deal of official landlord consternation about the van being parked there for two days. Neal says his sources told him that Mr. Landlord called every government agency and person in the phone book to question in great panic what was happening.

"Naturally, he found out zip because no one knew anything about it. And you know how bureaucracies are. It worked great," Neal said. "There were all sorts of rumors in the neighborhood among realtors and rental agents, and we heard a couple people did move."

I guess this evil landlord was so frustrated he almost shot at the van when Neal and friends finally went to return it, their mission accomplished. I guess that old boy couldn't have been more upset if Idi Amin had sat on his wife's face. Then again . . .

LAND RAPISTS

The Kangaroo Rat had a one-sided quarrel with some rich, agribusiness nasties who were taking water from real people and piping it to their lush farms several miles away. Their barristers were richer and far more politically influential than the dusty-suited lawyer the little people could afford, so I'm sure you know who won that courtroom charade.

The Rat took to hunting in the desert area around the water pipe, and when he fired at a rabbit or grouse, he usually missed and his 12-gauge shotgun's charge of #2 buckshot tore huge holes in the bad guys' water pipe.

I bet he felt guilty and stopped right there to patch up that pipe so that *no* leaks occurred. (I guess I lost that bet.) Thus, the water no longer was stolen from the river for awhile.

Doesn't everyone hunt small game with #2 buckshot? I recall in another life when some of us had to hunt larger game who were also hunting us. I found #2 buckshot a very appropriate load.

That's been an unsolicited hunting tip on behalf of #2 buckshot. It made me feel so good that I've decided to make a major cash contribution to the National Rifle Association in the name of several anti-gun asshole newspaper people from a major Eastern city. The funniest part is that it's their money.

They're welcome.

LAUNDRY

At one time, Kansas City's Ray Heffer patronized a certain coin-operated laundromat, as it was nearby one of his businesses. He ran into drug deals, homeless bums and drunks sleeping in dryers, violent, crazed panhandlers . . . and this place was in a fairly nice section of town.

He complained to the manager when his clothes were stolen right in front of him by an apparent friend of the manager. The manager laughed. Ray smiled ruefully, left, then got back.

"I placed several thin, nonreturnable beer bottles in each dryer," Ray said. "Nobody paid me any attention. I put in my coins, started the dryers, and moved smartly and quickly out of there, never to return."

The glass will churn around, break and pulverize, and then pieces will fall though the vent holes in the drum and down into the drive mechanism. Ray said a repair engineer suggested this to him as "a real bitch to repair." Time is money, Ray figures, and if people can't be at least semi-polite when robbing you, then they need to pay another way.

Ray, this Bud's on them.

LAWNS

Although no slave to his lawn, RLS of Apple Valley does expect privacy to do what he enjoys doing, when and how he wishes to do so. That's why he got really upset when a neighbor allowed his bitch and her pups—and I refer to the neighbor's dog here, not his family—to frolic in RLS's yard.

One of their major frolics was to dislodge, chew, and play-rip with RLS's carefully implanted soaker hose. After the pups and mom had torn apart two hoses, and the human neighbors appeared to be oblivious to the situation, RLS had a shocking idea.

"I did the entire project in very careful steps, despite being pissed as hell about how unconcerned the puppies' owners were. Anyway . . . ."

His first step was to water his lawn deeply, as in a good soaking. He *really* poured the water to it.

His next step was to leave his remaining soaker hose extended to its full fifty-foot length, then to run a thick twelve-gauge electrical wire all of the way through the inside of it. If we call that line the positive lead, do you get the idea what's going to happen?

Next, he stuck a steel spike in the ground and attached a wire to it. We'll call this the negative line. If this hasn't become clear yet, please read on to the next selection.

He then went back to the ends of the wire, attached them to a 110-watt wall outlet male plug, and waited for the fun.

When the little animal visitors came in for a close-up and their teeth closed down through the soaker hose and into the "hot" wire, the result made for action and noise. (That is why you really wet down the grass.)

This won't kill the animals, but it won't make them very happy either.

LAWYERS

It's not often that some common kid comes up from the ranks of the state college system with manure on his shoes and honesty in his heart to become a lawyer. Most come from the privileged class, and most went to prestigious law schools financed by their kin.

Literate American lawyer Clarence Darrow said that the trouble with law is lawyers. And as my old friend and former family lawyer, R. Westlake Bork, used to say, "The Ivy League upper class law school graduates make the best gangsters because they've had the most practice."

On the other hand, my current lawyer, Pene Orina, is so clever that he could walk into a courtroom in Tel Aviv and in ten minutes get the charges against Adolf Hitler reduced to littering. I wonder if old Pene still eats babies for breakfast? (I'm only joking. Those were pork umlauts he ate when we were on a legal study mission in Cabo San Lucas.)

Pene told me about a lawyer friend of his—a former partner—who had messed up his life and their partnership with drink and easy women. The guy became more than a liability and nearly cost Pene his career.

"I got him out, but that wasn't all I wanted," Pene told me. "I waited another year while this stewbum followed his dick through the singles bars and made a horrible reputation for himself."

Pene explained that the guy kept semisolvent by taking sure-pay, sure-lose drug cases, plus some estate work that brought in a modest amount of money for no mental effort (i.e., his loyal secretary carried him).

"My big payback was this," Pene said. "He finally got a case that could have won him some prestige and made him some serious money—never mind what or where. The judge was a solid puritan, probably still a virgin, and married to a professional virgin . . . no sense of humor, totally dry people," Pene told me.

"I had a pal who hired a whore—a real flashy one—to come on to the judge in the presence of his wife at a bar association retreat. She was primed and well paid to say she was a gift from . . . who else, but my former partner. The real joker is that my former partner had purposely stayed away from this party to build his reputation back."

Do you have to wonder about the outcome? If so, Pene reports that his former partner is now out of the law business and is trying to make a living as a political aide in Washington. He surely has all of the qualifications.

LETTERS

If you're lucky, says Tommie Titmouse, your mark will have written you a letter on some official business on personal letterhead. Using his letterhead logo, get a cooperative print shop in another town to print blank copies of the mark's letterhead for you. If you're on a tight budget, cut the letterhead logo off the mark's letter and use it in a top-quality copy machine to create the stationery yourself.

Step two is obvious; you're going to "become" your mark and write all sorts of bizarre letters to important and sensitive people. (By the way, use a public typewriter that you can rent at a copy store or public library in another town . . . or use the typewriter of a secondary mark.)

Following are some possibilities for the contents of these letters:

• Write really weird shit in a letter to the editor in the mark's local newspaper (e.g., "I am Thor's host in this life and believe in human sacrifice and sexual relations with children and house pets"). Stuff like that.

• Send cleverly worded blackmail letters to important people, noting that you have evidence that makes them guilty of fraud, drug use, sexual misconduct, being liberal, or whatever. In this case, be subtle enough to make it seem real.

• Write to militant ethnic and minority groups and offer to kick their asses. In this one, you could make your mark be a skinhead or other antagonist. As opposed to offering to fight, offer them oral or anal sex.

• Via your letters "from" the mark, get said mark involved on all sides of various social issues (e.g., gun control, Contra aid, abortion, pornography, civil rights). These letters should go to the authorities, editors, and powerful people of the local and state establishment.

And, as I suggested in an earlier book, you could also write threatening letters to people, especially people in the public eye. Thank you, Tommie Titmouse, for helping us to help our mark gain notoriety, attention, and entire new groups of people with whom he or she will now become acquainted. I guess this now makes our mark a man or lady of letters.

LOCKS

Security is important to all of us, and sometimes a lock is all that stands between us and the bad animals. If your mark has such a lock protecting something vital and important, you may wish to render that lock greatly useless. Think beyond the material damage and ponder the personal desecration.

I once knew a mark who had some valuable and time-perishable materials behind a heavy safe door in an otherwise untouchable room. It was decided (note the bureaucratic and nondirective use of passive voice) to render that lock useless, and thus make the room almost impossible to enter without grand, expensive technology. Following are the steps used:

• Select a one-sixteenth titanium drill bit.

• Dip the bit into a tube of liquid metal and coat it most generously.

• Insert the coated bit into the key channel of the lock and push it steadily home with a pen or nail head. When it comes home to battery, snap it off flush with the key channel face using heavy pliers.

• However, if your drill bit has fallen into the tumblers but you can still penetrate the key channel, coat another length of drill bit and repeat the process.

At this point, the door lock won't be opened for business as usual. Suffice to say that this door is secure!

The Green Weenie also had a problem with locks. He belonged to a cheap health club that had terrible maintenance policies and even less ethical or legal concern about security.

"I had a solid lock on my locker when I went for a shower," Green Weenie reported. "When I came back, some thief had simply jammed open my locker door without touching my lock. That's how cheap the entire hardware was."

Semiwrapped in a tiny towel, Green Weenie went to the lobby to complain to the management. In that and other contacts he was told, in effect, "Too fucking bad, pal. Sue us."

Green Weenie is doing that and more. As he reported, "I didn't want other folks to get their stuff ripped off, so I took some of those neat dual-hypo containers of epoxy and went on an inspection tour of the locker area to find defective lockers. I used the epoxy to seal these lockers permanently . . . to protect other members, of course."

It is comforting to me that I know such a civic-minded and selfless man as the Green Weenie. Somehow I can just picture a Norman Rockwell cover of Weenie on the old *Saturday Evening Post* protecting our locker room by sealing shut all of the lockers.

MAGAZINES

Here's a switch on the old gag of giving your mark ten thousand magazine subscriptions. And I want to thank my old law enforcement friend, Chief Retrete Gates from California, for sharing it with us. Thanks, you old son of a gun.

It happened in Medina, Ohio, early in 1989. A merry citizen with a difference ordered magazine subscriptions by the dozens for a group of city officials. The hook was that it appeared as if Official A was giving gift subscriptions to Official B, who appeared to be giving gift subscriptions to Official C, and so on. It's best described as a circle jerk, obviously, and it will come full cycle when the bills arrive. Happy reading, Medina.

Can you do the same thing for some of your least-favorite personalities or friends? Can you read? Can you write? And finally, dare you?

MARK

As in my other books, I use the word *mark* to refer to the object of your revenge. A mark can be a person, institution, company, animal, object—just about anything that has hurt you in any manner or continues to do so. Usually, you've tried all of the usual ethical, legal, moral, and Golden Rule things to make everyone happy. You're a paragon of patience, a vigor of virtue. But, your mark is a true anus stain and won't stop bullying, annoying, or bothering you.

This is when you begin to get angry. You're getting so frustrated and angry that you want to watch a rabid moray eel eat the mark's eyeballs . . . while the mark's still alive. Or you feel as if your mark needs to be in the nearest morgue's intensive care unit.

Hold those thoughts, because that's when it's time to call on George Hayduke, bullybuster. Within the pages of this book, you'll discover all sorts of bullybusting ideas, ranging from the mildly sardonic to the bombastically devastating.

But, as a matter of early warning intelligence, how can you spot a potential mark? Thanks to some exhaustive research at the Hayduke Institute of Semiological Research, Dr. Bruno McManmon, project director, has come up with some characteristics that fit a computer-generated model to profile myriad marks. This profile indicates that a potential mark:

- thinks that when she/he defecates, the odor of lilacs

fills the stall;

- is the sort of person for whom it would be redundant to claim ignorance;
- often carries that rotten-guilty look, like a nasty little boy who's peed his pants;
- has all of the sexual appeal of rancid lard;
- has a foul personality that stands out like a neon cockroach in a bowl of grits;
- blows dead bears for a quarter and gives change;
- would sell his/her grandmother to a Nigerian brothel if the price was right;
- has the personality of week-old sinus drainage;
- has the ethical standards of a Bolivian drug dealer selling poisoned heroin to kids in your neighborhood.

I could go on, but I suspect you get the drift. A mark is someone you want to come down on to make your neighborhood a nicer place to live. Nothing wrong with that.

Marks are all around us, unhappily, although there are statistically so few of them. It's your choice whether to respond to or ignore your mark. As the offended, you must choose who to fricassee on the hot coals of their ill-chosen act or words. So, to all of the marks in your life, I offer a curse from an old shaman I knew in another life in a dark, evil section of a small island south of the United States:

"The death fart from a terrified adult is
a thousand times worse than anything a live
body can emit. May such a death fart multiply
a thousand times in the nostrils of your enemy."

— Moloch Beelzebub
Hinchazon Cay, 1980

106

MICROWAVES

It isn't everyday that you can turn one of these kitchen miracles against your mark. But Rev. Willy did it for a very good reason. One of his in-laws borrowed some heavy bucks to buy a microwave, pledging to pay it back.

Willy recalls ruefully, "I waited and waited for my money. Nothing. When I asked about it, the skunk said he'd told other family members I had *given* him that money. He actually smirked at me and said, 'you wouldn't want to make a liar out of me.'

"I collected some roadkill and held them at my place until I knew he was going to do some cooking for guests. While he was outside checking drinks, I snuck in the side door, removed his roast from my money's microwave, and substituted a large, ripe, and dead groundhog. I took his roast, ran out the door, and went back to my place to enjoy his dinner."

Willy said he found out that the mark had no idea what was steaming away in the microwave until the steam and heat pressure built up inside the dead animal's skin and KAAAWHOOMMMMM . . . it exploded inside the oven, blowing open the door and spraying liquid yuck all over the kitchen.

"And, I had an iron alibi . . . I had my mother over to dinner at my place that evening and then we went bowling. Mom was my witness."

MILITARY

Face it, the business of the military is war. War is more profitable than peace. It is also more violent, which appeals to a lot of people. Some even say war is fun. I guess that all depends on how you came out of it.

War, you see, gives people free license for violence, which liberates the dark side of human nature. As the profound pacifist, screenwriter, and ex-GI Fred Rexer once noted, "Only brute force deserves respect, and the meek shall inherit the earth only when we're finished with it and with them."

That's telling those wimpy little shits, Fred!

I liked the military and managed to "retire" quite honorably with a sergeant's rank. Former Major Jim Morris, another of us who is not growing up, merely aging, asked me the other day if the military still sings raunchy Jody or cadence songs.

Jody songs were just an early form of rap music, I think. Indeed, Morris told me that some chap actually wrote and had published an entire book of Jody songs. One of the best Jody verses I ever laughed at was shared with me by the Peeking Sage from Stillwater, himself yet another vet:

> *"A yellow bird with a yellow bill*
> *was sitting on my window sill;*
> *coaxed him in with a piece of bread;*
> *then I crushed his fucking head ..."*

You know the rest, "Sound off, etc." Thanks for that one, old Peekin' Sage. But, I digress. I am not speaking of today's modern army, where they have M16A2 rifles with training wheels and comic book manuals because the all-volunteer grunts are too fucking illiterate to read real manuals. As with all old farts, I speak fondly of the old days.

I wasn't used to being around headquarters, and there were always enough heavy metal types—brass variety—around to make any peon under the rank of major very nervous. The military, you see, operates as a major caste system. But there I was, thinking, "Wow, there's enough brass around here to cast a dozen or so good-sized spit-toons." But it's also where I heard about this great stunt.

I heard it from Corporal Scales, who'd been in since Korea and had never risen above E-5. For all the usual reasons, he'd been up and down the line of Article 15 through the lower-level courts. Anyway, he was telling me how it went after his first tour.

"We were back from the field, and wouldn't you know it, the showers were out. The guys were pissed, and so was our first shirt, who bitched to the CO," Scales told me.

"The CO made some phone calls and proclaimed that the showers would be on in one hour. He then proceeded to his own home (a nice cushy pad, as we soon found out) just off post.

"No showers in one hour, let alone the whole night. The first sergeant stayed with us—I'll give him that—in that stinking Deep South summer heat. The same damn thing the next day—the post engineers don't show.

"Not only that, but the CO runs us ragged, says we're still in training and not to whine. We even had to dry shave —dry except for the constant sweat. But, no sweat for the

109

CO—he's got a shower. Man, we stink. We are unhappy. . . very unhappy. The top soldier and the CO have some kind of heated powwow behind closed doors, but the clerk says the CO pledged that the men would have showers that night.

"Well, the CO obviously had no pull, as we got no showers. That's when the first sergeant called a company formation and told our platoon sergeants to fall out, each man with his towel and shower gear.

"We were formed into ranks and marched in perfect military order right out the main gate and down a highway, then about two miles into some civilian streets, until we were right in front of the CO's house. We were halted while the first sergeant went up to the CO's door , knocked and informed the CO's wife that he and the men were here to honor the officer's pledge for each man to have a shower that night."

Scales said the officer was dumbstruck. The sergeant said they'd start with the lower ranks in alphabetical order. He started to call out names. The flustered officer stopped him and begged for a moment.

"Shit, within ten minutes we were told trucks were coming for us, and we were taken back to the post and sent to the gymnasium for showers. We were then trucked back to our company area. Engineers were just finishing fixing our showers," Corporal Scales told me.

He said the CO was relieved several weeks later and was sent to an outpost in the Aleutian Islands. The first sergeant was given a promotion and later assigned to a tour in Germany (which, back in the early '60s, when this took place, was a vacation).

There is something called military justice . . . .

THE MOB

My good friend Scimunitos Blatta told me not to even think about picking on the mob. Says he, "George, they'll come down on you like a meat cleaver smashing a mouse, and that's just their lawyers." I assured him that I had no intention of doing that. Instead, I was going to relate how good old Piper Pub made use of the mob in his scheme to pay back a deadbeat ex-friend who'd stiffed him on a personal loan, then bad-mouthed him in town.

"Many times, pizza shops are owned by mob figures as a front operation, local money laundry, or to give the button guys a semireal job for IRS cover. I know of a wonderful twist whereby a mark who did you in could end up like the poor *noid* in those clever commercials for a real straight pizza outfit that's not mob connected," Piper explains.

Piper's stunt works like this. You call the mob-connected pizza place and order six or eight pizzas. Be sure to include a couple with anchovies, as they don't keep well and shouldn't be reheated. You ask them how long this will take, as you have a dozen hungry friends at your place after a concert, ball game, or whatever.

They tell you forty-five minutes. You say OK and place the order (using a pay phone, of course). You use the name and address of your mark when placing the order. Give the pizza place the number of the pay phone. Naturally, they'll call back to confirm your order, thinking they're talking to your mark.

Anxiously, but politely, you say, "Well yes, of course it

111

was I who called. Please hurry, we're starved and your pizza is so good."

Wait five minutes and call again to check on your order. How much longer, maybe add some fries, whatever. Hang up. Call again about ten minutes later. Be a bit more insistent this time. Get a bit huffy. Wait five minutes and call again.

"Start out polite, then within ten seconds blow your top at their incompetence, dishonesty, and bad phone manners. Demand to speak to the night manager. When he or she gets on the phone, really let loose. Use ethnic intimidation, racial slurs, sexual threats, then tell 'em you're going to come down there and burn them out or blow up the place," Piper says.

The finale is to tell them that you (you are, of course, using the mark's name) are in real tight with the local Godfather, whom you know owns that shop. Really be abusive. Scream. Tell them you're on your way in to cut the balls off of the Godfather and slice 'em up for someone else's pizza.

See, I told you it was funny.

MOOCHERS

As the Bronx Bomber says to me, it's amazing you don't get more complaints about moochers or, as he also calls them, borrow-sharks. He notes that they're always, borrowing just a little of this or that and, if you're not around, just taking it anyway.

He's correct, and the worst part is that these are not close friends until they need something from you or me. His first thought was to do them in with planted drugs, but that is expensive and hysterically illegal now.

Aquarium gravel, however, is quite legal and also cheap. Sprinkling some into a tasty chocolate cake or other such recipe will produce some grand results. He says to leave pieces of the cake available for the moochers and sharks.

Another suggestion for moocher protection came from Cracked Commode, who says you should always loan someone else's something to these leeches.

"But you don't tell the original owner that you're loaning something of his or hers to the moocher," he cautions. "Only after the property is in the moocher's possession do you alert the owner in a roundabout way."

The kicker is that owner will think a robbery has taken place. You, of course, have already distanced yourself from this entire situation by going on a vacation or business trip. If asked when you return, Cracked Commode said your response is a blank look followed by "Who? What? I don't follow you. What are you talking about?"

NATIONAL PARKS

Another frightening federal program against environmental activists was the FBI blitzkrieg against several Earth First! leaders in May of 1989. Following the orders of their rich corporate masters, George Bush's fascist forces took the land-preservation activists to prison in true police-state style.

Others have been threatened, visited, and placed under investigation and/or surveillance—including your obedient servant, me, myownself. In response, I would like to offer a peaceful, positive alternative to all of the negative, destructive measures.

Let's increase the size of our state and national parks. Currently, the only way you, we, or the Feds know where the park border happens to be is because someone has put up a sign or wire designating that as the border. Sounds arbitrary to me.

Consider the maps. Most are based either on ancient—really ancient—survey lines, on someone's memory, or on arbitrary decision. What I'm saying is that in most states and many national parks, nobody really knows where the *true* borders are.

Hence, here's my idea. To keep the land rapists off balance, why not move the park borders outward? Either move the National Forest Service signs outward a couple hundred yards (which is probably a felony these days, thanks to Asshole I and Asshole II, our past and immediate presidents) or create newly printed boundary signs, get rid of the old ones, and put up yours.

You can do the same thing for state parks. Perhaps it would even work for county or local parks, I don't know. It's certainly worth a try.

It's just an idea, but I like it.

NEIGHBOR

Sometimes it snows fairly heavily where Uncle Gerry and Rusty live. They have some very inconsiderate neighbors in their neck of the woods as well. Combine the two, and, well, let's let Rusty finish the story.

"This creep of a neighbor just left his car in the street outside his house, barely off the road because he's too lazy to shovel his driveway. That made it really tough for Ger or me to get our car out of our shoveled driveway, plus the hog's car was blocking the road.

"Later that night (while it was still snowing so our tracks would be covered), Uncle Gerry and I ripped the license plate right off this guy's car, which was a few years old and not all that new and shiny. Then, we did our duty as good citizens and reported an abandoned car that was blocking traffic. We gave the police only the block address.

"The police showed up. With no license plate number to check, they assumed the car had indeed been abandoned, plus we told them it had been there all week. They called a tow truck and had the car towed off to the pound.

"It was great watching Mr. Creep the next morning go through a coronary-inducing panic routine. It took him and the police two days to locate his car, and there was a hefty fine for getting it out of the pound.

"He sued the city over the incident and spent about eight hundred dollars in legal fees. He lost the case. There is justice," Rusty said, breaking into his barking laugh.

A case related by Piper Pub is not as amusing, until

right before the end, when our hero triumphs. His friend's neighbors were true genetic drift, a mutant cross between swamp gas and the worst of an incestuous tryst between the Juke and Manson families. They had what passed for two sons and a daughter.

Piper says, "To catalog the evil and awful deeds they committed against my friend—their neighbor—would fill another book. Let's just say that the local cops were afraid of these animals. No amount of legal complaining worked, which is why I got involved."

Piper, who works as a garbage collector in the true Hayduke sense, located some of the one boy's schoolwork in the trash. Actually, they were illiterate ramblings that had earned an F in a high school remedial English class.

"I changed all of that," Piper says with a twist of Miltonian humor. "I recreated the messages so that they would be sexual love poetry to his mother and father that degenerated into pitiful pleas for help."

Piper made it appear that the kid thought this incestual stuff was wrong, but that his parents had taught it to him and sometimes he enjoyed it . . . . The rest, which was quite explicit, I leave to your vivid imagination.

Next, Piper took the rewritten material, in its erotic, psychopathic state, plus a sample of the original paper in the kid's own handwriting, to a friend who was a state-certified forger (i.e., he'd done time for it).

"That's right," Piper added. "We did that family in. My friend used the kid's handwriting to recreate my porno poetry and plea for help from this kid."

The poem was then mailed to a local right-wing fundamentalist preacher, who was also obnoxious, according to Piper. The preacher's secretary, who opened all of the mail, was a three-hundred-pound telecommunications marvel. Piper said she could spread rumors through that town faster than FAX!

The result? The Dreaded Duo of Ma and Pa spent so much time with authorities and in juvie court that they didn't have time to be evil to Piper's pal. They also moved away from the area because they were on the state and county law enforcement people's shitlist, as are all child molesters, innocent or guilty.

"The irony of honesty here is that some of the stuff turned out to be true," Piper told me. "The old lady had been playing with the kid in a nasty way for about four years, and he liked it. The old man was an unhappy person about that, too."

Ira from New Rochelle had a clod of a next-apartment neighbor who worked the night shift. He clomped in with his heavy boots (no carpets), opened and slammed shut the refrigerator door, gulped two beers, and belched like a jet afterburner at 1:00 A.M. Then he clomped into the bedroom — separated from Ira's apartment by only a thin wall — tossed his boots loudly to the floor and began to make loud, sloppy lust with his noisy girlfriend.

Ira adds, "I'm in the next apartment trying to sleep, with my bed only three feet from this animal and only a thin wall between us. I needed to sleep, as I had to work at six in the morning. This went on six nights a week."

When Ira asked the man for some consideration, he was threatened physically. Here is what Ira did in response.

With a borrowed key, he let himself into the empty apartment directly under the loud neighbor's place. He removed the light fixture directly under the clod's bedroom and replaced it with a fifteen-inch speaker attached to a two-hundred-watt amplifier and a Spotmaster deck, which is a tape-loop (continuous play) unit.

The tape in question was a recording of various howitzer blasts. Ira waited until the hump was in bed and as soon as he heard the loud lady approaching a climax, he hit the ON button.

"Actually, the howitzer blasts were not quite as loud as the confusion, fear, and consternation upstairs. I played it for three minutes, then quickly removed my stuff and replaced the light fixture. I hid my gear in a lockable closet and waited under the bed of the abandoned apartment," Ira reports.

Sure enough, within five minutes a very shaken couple and the super came in to see what was happening. The super made a cursory inspection, told the man and woman they were dreaming, and grumped back to his own bed.

Ira says that it took only two more howitzer attacks until the couple moved out.

NEWSPAPERS

Someone with access to publishing equipment, time, a sense of humor, and some healthy money spoofed the somewhat liberal *Arizona Daily Star* early in 1989 by placing five hundred copies of a phony front page in that newspaper's vending machines. The bogus page dealt with a U.S. military invasion of El Salvador, claiming seventy thousand casualties. It was, of course, a major hoax on the Tucson newspaper.

The pranksters carefully duplicated the newspaper's regular front page from the fold up, including use of the masthead, ears, and layout/typography style. It was a professional job. Credit for the stunt was claimed by the "Wednesday Morning Coffee Club of Tucson." A political diatribe was included on the page to the effect that the establishment media of Tucson were the accomplices of U.S. policies in Central America and not the watchdogs. (From my standpoint of having been in Central America on business quite often during the past decade, that charge is fairly accurate around most of the U.S. media centers.)

It may also help to explain the genesis of this great hoax by noting that Tucson is a center for the *Sanctuary* movement, which smuggles Central American war refugees into the U.S.

Ironically, the *Arizona Daily Star* has been a consistent critic of Reagan/Bush warmongering. The paper's managing editor, John Peck, said he thought the hoaxsters chose the paper not because of its editorial views but because it is well-respected and has wide circulation in the area.

It also has a sense of humor, I hope.

Speaking of a sense of humor, I had reason to become victoriously acquainted with a rather bellicose individual who is a newspaper editor. One of his staffers related an in-house joke about this newsroom dictator. It seems that after her annual checkup, a Sweet Young Thing told her gynecologist that she was concerned because some of her myriad boyfriends demanded anal sex.

"Can I get pregnant that way?" she asked.

"Of course you can," her doctor replied. "Where do you suppose newspaper executive editors come from?"

But, back to our story of other hoaxes. Where would another morning coffee club strike its blow for freedom of and from the press?

The answer came less than two weeks after the Tucson incident when the same basic stunt was pulled on the *Baltimore Sun*, a newspaper generally favorable to our last two reigning monarchs of the Right. In this instance, a group known as the Baltimore Emergency Response Network took public credit for the stunt, which brought out a fake *Sun* front page lambasting George Bush and the continuation of the harsh antipopulist Reagan policies in Central America.

In true establishment fashion, *Sun* publisher Reg Murphy oinked that the stunt was "a vile abuse of the First Amendment" and demanded a federal and local police investigation. He brought to mind that wonderful line by T.S. Eliot, "I suppose most editors are failed writers, but so are most writers."

The *Chicago Tribune* was not amused either when editorial hoaxers found them in March of '89. One of their executive suitmen stuffed his hairshirt and issued a statement reeking of corporate flatulence.

Milo Tinsnip needed to pay back an especially obnoxious newspaper editor for his Napoleonic cruelty. It's a given that while TV people are celebrities, newspaper people are for the most part totally unknown, sometimes even to their families and friends. Milo took advantage of this bit of truth.

"This little Hitler lived in a bedroom community and was as little-known in suburbia as he was in the city. The newspaper executive was a faceless nobody, and I got an actor friend to impersonate him," Milo told me.

His actor friend went to local meetings, identified himself as the editor, and was really gross, arrogant, and subversive. He was cruel, profane—in brief, a hateful character. He did this all week while the real mark was out of town on vacation. Then, the actor split. Mr. Editor/Mark had a very interesting homecoming.

As popular media target Angela Davis observed far more bluntly more than twenty years ago, "America is a whorehouse, and the media are its piano players."

PAINT

I have outlined many uses for paint and many vehicles and methods of delivery systems over the years. So I can't believe I have forgotten to mention such a grand product as the paint guns used by survivalists and others who use them for their little war games.

There are paint pistols, rifles, automatic weapons, and grenades. My God, what amazing possibilities these bring to my mind. And you don't really have to use the safe, water-soluble paints usually sold for the guns. You can get real paint, too. Or, as Captain Video suggests, use a hypodermic syringe to suck the paint out of the little balls, then use another syringe to refill each with another substance (e.g., urine, thinned-out vomit, Hershey squirts or other runny diarrhea, odor of skunk, deer musk, chicken liquid, and so on).

Captain Video brought this omission to my attention. So, a round (no pun) of applause for the good captain. As to the uses of this information, beyond those knowing, rotten/dirty chortles and yucks I hear out there, you're on your own.

These paint guns and supplies are carried by many sporting goods stores and departments. They are also available by mail order, so check ads in military, gun, and survival magazines.

PORNOGRAPHY

When you really want to hassle a mark, there is nothing like the old S&M-style porn to rub in the wrong message. Yes, you can use the whips-and-welts crowd to get back at your mark, and here's how.

It isn't just our decadent society, of course. According to the *China Daily News*, in the summer of 1989, a publishing house in western China was inadvertently binding twenty pages of a pornographic novel into elementary school grammar textbooks. According to a government report from Beijing, the stunt occurred because a dissatisfied worker decided to take revenge upon his communist masters. He said it was his protest against their social censorship. He was reprimanded and made to work for a year without salary. It's to his benefit that he was a productive worker; had he been a protesting student he probably would have been run down by a tank, or even worse (gasp), by the ultimate of evils, an AK47 *assault rifle.*

Meanwhile, in the porn wars, The Wall has a suggestion that will work for just about any mark, although he used this specifically against some real snotsuckers with whom he had to work in a professional office. He says it was a very snooty, gossipy place.

"I watched the mailboxes of two of the assholes who made my life miserable for no other reason than I was younger than they were. Over a month's time, I swiped a few of their professional magazines that came to the office.

"I carefully removed the mailing labels, then just as carefully glued them to some really sleazy, demented sex magazines. I replaced the magazines I'd been stealing with the porno publications. I spread this out for two months.

"The two people were frantic in their denials to co-workers who jagged them without mercy. Finally, the boss mentioned something to them about personal mail at the office. You know, nobody even thought of little old me, back in the shadows being Mr. Quiet."

As other options, the Wall says you could also put the sex magazines with the mark's mailing label in other workers' mailboxes, or forward them to the mark's home address or to the parents' address. Or, forward them to the boss, the CEO, or the CEO's spouse.

A letter from a Mr. Tupada noted that his favorite marks are the leaders of the professional antiporn police, like the Ayatollah of Tupelo, the Reverend Donald Wildmon, who is a very, very dangerous fascist.

On the other hand, there are some Quayles . . . errr, I mean clowns . . . in this organized bowel movement who want to rid the nation of its First Amendment freedoms. One, a Dr. James Fopson, with a straight face—if empty mind—defined autoeroticism as "an evil, demented practice." Gee, I thought it meant using a key to turn on your car.

Another leading citizen for decency who spoke at a public meeting I attended said that he was disturbed when he saw old back issues of *Colliers* at flea markets because they often used pictures of "scanty-clad starlets" on the cover. He said his name was Emil Cafone and he was ready to torch any store selling pornography.

Somewhere down in hell, Torquemada and his ilk must be smiling at the plans of their successors up here.

POST OFFICE

I used to live in a little town called Gazetteland, where it seems that to qualify to be a window clerk at the local post office you had to have the disposition of a cranky moray eel and the personality of a boil. I'm sure you know the type—someone who gives misanthropy a bad name. My friend Lisa Flema struck back one day.

It seems one of the dour sourballs forced himself to sell Lisa some stamps, muttering as he did so. He shoved the stamps across the counter at her and they fell to the dirty floor. The man just stared; not a word came from his nasty, welded lips.

Good old Lisa bent down, picked up the stamps, and put them in her purse, from which she took out the exact change for the stamps and placed it in the exact same spot on the floor. She walked out without a word.

It wasn't too long ago that the USPS itself suggested a wonderful idea for obtaining free postage at least part of the time. A letter to me from a friend arrived with its stamp torn off—somewhere, I guess, in a branch post office. The local officials there duly—or dully—used a rubber stamp to affix the following legend on the spot where the stamp had been: "EVIDENCE OF STAMP HAVING BEEN AFFIXED." It was in that special purple/maroon ink they favor for official postal proclamations.

My first step was to check with Billy Ortega, my local postal magnate and former lead guitarist for Deb & Her Great Buns, a senior citizen rock group. Billy explained to me that the inked proclamation meant that the stamp had either fallen off the letter or been lost, and that meant the letter could be delivered without postage. He also thought anyone could get such an ink stamp created somewhere and could probably also match the shade of the USPS ink.

Someone could, I guess, obtain the necessary items to experiment with this idea. I suspect it is a felony to attempt postal fraud. Usually, people who operate the post office have little sense of humor. I mean, you've been in one of their shops haven't you? They are hardly the boutique on the mall when it comes to guffaw.

QUOTES

As I do in each of my books, I am including wonderfully fine and funny quotes that are available for you to use in your life.

These quotes make fine philosophy for your own peace of mind, are creative thoughts to muse upon, or can be used as graffiti or custom bumper stickers. They also make great lines to spice your conversation.

• "I LOVE HELL. I CAN'T WAIT TO GET BACK."
> -Malcolm Lowry

• "A CREATURE WHO KEEPS A SHARP LOOKOUT AND ACTS PRUDENTLY ALL OF HIS LIFE OFTEN ENJOYS THE PLEASURE OF TRIUMPHING OVER MEN OF SUPERIOR IMAGINATION."
> -Stendahl (née Marie Henri Beyle)

• "ENJOYMENT MUST BE MEASURED BY PERSONAL ACCOMPLISHMENT AGAINST ONE'S ENEMIES."
> -Lupero Deracinate

• "IT IS BETTER TO DEBATE A QUESTION WITHOUT SETTLING IT THAN TO SETTLE A QUESTION WITHOUT DEBATING IT."
> -Joseph Joubert

• "THE WRATH OF THE LION IS THE WIS-
DOM OF GOD."
                    -William Blake

• "MY CAR EXPLODES ON IMPACT!"
                    -Michael Spinks

• "KILL THE YUPPIE SCUM!"
                    -Bob and Michelle Wells

• "GIVE TO THE PROSTITUTES' RELIEF
FUND. THEY GAVE TO YOURS."
                    -The Rev. Ayatollah Wilkins
                    Citizens for Decency

• "I'LL TRADE YOU THREE OF MY FIELD
HANDS FOR A LID OF YOUR BEST HEMP."
-Thomas Jefferson to George Washington

• "IF NIETZSCHE ISN'T DEAD YET, I'LL SEE
THAT HE IS."
                    -LTC Oliver North (USMC, Ret.)

• "ECOLOGY IS FOR THE BIRDS."
                    -James Watt

• "EXCUSE US FOR BEING UNGRATEFUL
FOR THE PUBLICITY."
                    -Sacco & Vanzetti

• "I DON'T KNOW WHETHER TO KILL
MYSELF, WATCH TV, OR GO BOWLING."
                    -Mrs. Joe Sixpack

• "HOW CAN WHISKEY ONLY SIX YEARS OLD BEAT UP SO BAD ON A GROWN MAN?"
-Willie Nelson

• "I'LL CLEAN UP MY ROOM, MAKE MY BED, EAT MY VEGETABLES, AND PROMISE TO BE A GOOD LITTLE GUY IF YOU'LL LET ME BE SECRETARY OF DEFENSE."
-Li'l John Tower

• "SHE WAS SO HORNY THAT SHE USED TO SIT ON SPEAKERS WITH THE BASS TURNED WAY UP SO SHE COULD GET OFF."
-Terri Lee

RADIOS

Ira from New Rochelle has taught me new uses for CB and ham radios. He once lived next to a real hardcase bastard who cut Ira's transmitter lines, tossed garbage in Ira's cans, and let his kids run in Ira's garden. He also worked on his ugly, loud car at night.

"When he got an automatic garage door opener for his flip-up door—not the rolling-up type of door—I knew I had him," Ira says. "I could use my radio to open or close his door. When he turned out all the lights I gave him twenty minutes, then tuned my radio to channel 5A on the 11-meter band and opened his door for him.

"He came out bitching and shut the door. I gave him ten minutes and did it again. He bitched at the door and its salesman even more. Ten more minutes, I opened it again. But this time I closed it on him while he was still inside the garage with the light out. He had to open the window and scream for his wife to let him out of the unattached garage. You'd better believe she was pissed, and she gave him hell for getting the door in the first place."

But Ira's topper came two days later when Mr. Mark was tooling into his driveway after having activated the door open. He was talking with his wife and not watching.

"Using my radio, I closed it on him, and he hit the door when it was only three feet from being fully closed. He drove clear through the damn door. Man, was he steamed," Ira says.

RATS

As I sat watching the third of Steven Spielberg's wonderfully entertaining *Indiana Jones* film trilogy, I noted that some of the loudest and most sincere "UGGGHHHS" and gut-felt "YUUUUCKS" were gasped out during the scenes with the rats. Even the snakes and bugs didn't get as much negative audience attention as the rats.

Piper Pub must have had this in mind when he suggested the use of rats to infest an neighborhood, building, room, car, or some other environment or person connected with it that you have reason to dislike to the point of revenge.

"Don't get the docile pet shop or lab permutations," Piper cautions. "You want those huge, evil wharf rats that live in the parts of town where even the babies don't taste good to them."

You can either pay local denizens twenty-five cents per rat or trap them yourself. Be sure to get more females than males, as we're going to use nature to increase your bounty of furry gifts to your former environment.

Personally, Piper had lived in a mean neighborhood of mean people who were semiliving proof of genetic drift. When he departed, he thought he should dress up his old neighborhood by bringing in a better class of resident.

Hence . . . Piper adds, "When you deliver your new citizens, be sure to quietly and gently tip over a few garbage cans in the midst of the night to help these new chaps on their merry way. This gives them an idea of how to get their next meal."

As notorious for their sexual proclivity as their obnoxious appearance and social habits, the rats will naturally reproduce rapidly. This is a gift that just keeps on giving.

Perhaps that is what old Hubert Ledbetter meant when he mused, "Sometimes things get so terribly awful that you just hafta laugh and laugh." Then again, perhaps that's not what he meant. But Piper did; I'm laughing and I don't even like rats.

RELIGION

There are many types of religious leaders. Some are interested in their flock, while others seem intent only on fleecing their flock. On the other hand, if you tired years ago of some brainwashed robot holding up a sign saying "John 3:16" every time the TV camera focuses on a football sailing through the uprights, enjoy what the Gorch brothers are doing about it.

Taking the matter in hand, my old pals Lyle and Tector Gorch attended the 1989 NCAA Final Four in Seattle with their lady buddy Penelope Penophile. This madcap trio wore assorted custom-made t-shirts and baseball caps inscribed in Biblical script: "Genesis 38:8-10," "Knights of St. Onan," and "St. Onan Pray for Us."

Biblical scholars among you will, of course, recall Onan as the unhappy camper who, when directed to impregnate his brother's widow, instead chose to spread his seed on the ground, as the old biblical euphemism goes.

While the twelfth century scholar/philosopher Pene en Mano immortalized Onan by inventing the word onanism to refer to masturbation, too few young people are acquainted with Onan's significant contribution to the popular culture of Judeo-Christianity. That's where the Gorch brothers and their many friends have taken up the cudgel.

After returning from Seattle, the boys were kicking the gong around at the pleasant surprise they got from public reaction to their messages.

Lyle said, "We were stopped everywhere in Seattle—in

the Kingdome, bars, restaurants—by ordinary folks who wanted to know about St. Onan. When we explained who and what he was and why we were wearing the caps and shirts, we got overwhelming approval and a lot of laughs."

That the boys were out to ridicule the Bible-Thumpers, the John 3:16 crazies, and Do-As-I-Command Christians was obvious. What was grand was the happy response they got. A dozen Seton Hall students vowed to replicate the mission in South Orange, New Jersey. A University of Michigan professor said he thought Ann Arbor to be a fertile ground for expanding the movement and vowed to take the mission in hand.

The Gorch boys have only begun. Watch for their work during sports telecasts. If you should see a bearded mammoth holding up a sign for the TV cameras, look closely. It's Lyle or Tector with a sign that says "SATAN LIVES." Or, just behind one of the "John 3:16" assholes you might see one of the boys holding their banner, "LEVITICUS 20:13," or anything else to make trouble.

Tector has asked for your help. If you're in a ballpark and some cretin holds up his radical religious message, you can do the same thing using one of the Gorch messages, or you can locate and disseminate some of your own.

"Leviticus 20 is a gold mine of verses covering every sort of sexual aberration imaginable," Tector adds. "Many other chapters of Leviticus are good, as are much of Numbers, Deuteronomy, and the Song of Solomon."

RESERVOIR
OF REVENGE

Uncle Chris, one of the co-inventors of Carpball (see the *Fish* chapter), told me about how easy it would be to convince paranoid city officials that you'd nastied their water supply.

"All you'd need to do is lay some empty bags that had contained poison around the edge of a community water supply. You don't even have to climb the fence; just toss the empty bags over the fence near the water," Uncle Chris suggests.

There are all sorts of appropriate products that will do the trick, including agricultural pesticides, exterminator's chemicals, toxic dump bags, and the like. The secret is to be sure that nothing nasty actually gets in the water, of course, or the stunt could obviously backfire.

The same idea in somewhat modified form was suggested by Domini Stephanos, whose previous life was no doubt spent with the fun Yippies of the '60s. Those fun people (some of whom are today's stressed-out establishment leaders) convinced Chicago officials that they had put LSD in the city water supply by much the same methods.

Some things stay the same, including the identity of the civic bad guys, it seems.

Actually, this stunt may be rendered moot by the increase in acid rain pelting portions of the United States and Canada. Drinking water in these regions actually will make you light up and glow, I guess.

RESTAURANT

We were sitting on the balcony of my friend Claussen's quiet villa overlooking the Plaza de La Puta Virgin discussing rude restaurants. Tim asked Pearl about her last experience with a nasty eatery. She had a brief complaint about tough, cold food and a surly waiter with the manners of a pro hockey goon-enforcer.

"I grabbed a handful of their dinner mints and retired to the privacy of a stall in the lady's loo. I unwrapped each mint, took it out, and sucked on them some, being careful to also get some teeth marks on them.

"I rewrapped each used mint very carefully and replaced them in the bowl. I was hoping that a less quiet and uncomplaining customer than I would get these recycled mints," Pearl said.

Speaking of a grand bite out of your restaurant/mark, Doc Byte has a formula to help unflavor french fries. He says to drop in some amylase, which is an enzyme that breaks down starch and ruins the whole process.

"Or add some color by putting iodine in the french fry oil," Doc Byte suggests. "Don't mix the two; add one or the other. Either way, you upset everyone."

Storm Trooper's sister had an experience with the owner of a fast-food franchise restaurant who hired and fired with date-rape potential as his major criterion. This jerk was rarely in his restaurant but always expected perfection anyway. He was usually out balling some bimbo-in-training or trying to bribe/rape some innocent kid over a job.

"I could do his voice perfectly on the phone, so I would call a couple of his franchise restaurants and give the manager orders to run certain specials, order more of this and less of that, fire this person or that person, or close early, open late, stuff like that. It was great fun and worked really well," Storm Trooper reported.

From the impressive list of citations, legal actions, and visits from regulatory agency people responding to various complaints from former employees and the general public, I would agree that Storm Trooper did well.

As usual, Captain Video has a quiet counterpoint with equal bite to it. He suggests having a friendly, out-of-town printer use the logo of your mark/restaurant to print some official-looking coupons offering a free meal to Mr./Ms. Mark and three guests—their pick of the menu.

Use secondary marks for the distribution of these coupons, the captain suggests. At best, the police will be called; or almost as good, an unpleasant public scene will occur. The worst case scenario, according to the captain, would be if the restaurant, to avoid publicity, honored the coupons. (Of course, if you print more than a few, you will probably achieve the best case scenario.)

Then there was the Happy Clone Hostess in a really awful restaurant with death-slow service and bland tasteless food who dared to ask Sassy Sissy "was everything just wonderful, dearie?"

Sissy snarled back, "Your service here is just like an old elephant shits, dearie—slow and sloppy."

I was there. It was great.

ROOMIES

One of the best benefits to blasting a roommate is the ease of access. Of course, that also raises the personal complicity for you, the other roommate. Careful adherence to the Hayduke Commandments is urged, and don't let the concept of a strong alibi go asunder.

There is a literal buffet of stunts here. The Bronx Bomber suggests some fun mix-n-switch items like turpentine as shampoo (and no, the mark won't smell it until too late). There is also mineral oil for mouthwash, petroleum jelly as mascara, and turning Comet or Ajax into bath or deodorant powder.

You can also do things like grind eggshells up very well and put them into roomie's expensive running shoes. This makes for mini-discomfort . . . until it's too late. Think about those blisters.

If you room with a jock, try some fresh chewing gum jammed up into the toes of his/her athletic shoes. Or use peanut butter. Either stunt should place roomie on the emotional disabled list. The Bronx Bomber also suggests the same stunt using slime or one of the other yucky, gucky flowing messes. Alternatives for filling jock shoes include toothpaste, Vaseline, cosmoline mousse, shaving cream, and so on.

Remember, as I cautioned earlier, keep in mind that you are very, very exposed to both suspicion and retribution in these circumstances.

SCHOOL

Beezlenecks, geeks, intellectual bullies, and unscholarly jocks who cheated used to bug the Renegade. He complained about doing his best on his own and still coming in behind these cheaters. Nobody listened or cared. So he shut up for a term, then he sought help through forgery.

"Like most schools, we had midquarter progress reports sent to the home," the Renegade related. "I thought I could file more truthful ones about these unpunished cheaters than the school authorities sent, so I took one of my old ones and used white-out to cover the typed evaluations so that only the headings and title showed.

"Using a Xerox machine, I made blank copies of the form. I then used a school typewriter during a study period to prepare bogus reports for those moral criminals. I forged the appropriate signature and mailed them to the parents of the baddies."

The Renegade says the reaction was great and that there was an investigation. But he'd taken my suggested precautions so as not to fall under suspicion. He also reports much hard feeling between the families and school officials.

One of our Pennsylvania pen pals, the Wall, recently took very good care of one of the bullyjocks in his school. It was quite simple, which, of course, matched the mark, the Wall reported.

"The guy bullied everyone, including his coach, who had a lot of pull with the principal and school board," he added.

"I managed to get hold of a couple of his class notebooks. He had little written in his except girls' names and sexual fantasies . . . horrible speller, too. But his name was in each book in his own handwriting."

The Wall brought to school a bunch of hardcore gay porno magazines with muscular guys doing very explicit things to each other. He seeded these throughout the jock mark's notebooks.

"I then planted them in strategic locations around the school" (e.g., the prim librarian's desk, the school chaplain's waiting room, the security office, and the girls' locker room).

There was a hearing, a whole lot of publicity, embarrassment, and the like. Although he was found innocent, he was kicked off the football team for the season. The Wall says the guy became a great deal more human, too. Maybe there is something about education?

On the other side of that argument, a survey taken of graduating seniors at Dartmouth in 1989 showed that 48 percent knew what the acronym SDI stood for, while 76 percent knew what the acronym IUD meant. Priorities, folks, priorities—and who's to judge, right?

SMEGMA

My just and wise compatriot, Dick Smegma, is getting fan mail. With apologies to Sally Field, people *like* Dick Smegma—they really like him. I told you, he's a class person. So, rather than function as Dick's mail forwarding service, here is his own personal, direct address:

Dick Smegma
c/o P.O. Box 6291
Kahului, HI 96732-6291

In the meantime, here is a Smegma Special, the main ingredient of which is feces—one of his and my favorites for deserving folks. Dick says you have a bunch of fliers printed that advertise FREE FECAL ANALYSIS, with your promotional copy stressing the media-enriched topic of colon and rectal cancer and the importance of early testing.

You tell people that their samples will be analyzed privately and in strict confidence by highly experienced medical professionals in a modern lab facility. And tell them their individual analysis report will be returned to them in a plain letter.

Your flier should persuasively urge folks to mail a sample of their stool in a sealed plastic bag (giving brand name recommendations is a good touch) to the mark's home address. Of course, you use a fancy-sounding research or analytical laboratory as a business name, telling them to be sure to address it to the mark's attention.

The kicker is that your mark will receive many bags of

shit by mail. You can distribute these fliers at shopping centers, flea markets, or leave them on the "public service" tables of malls and markets.

SMOKE

Ever been in a situation where you needed to get away fast? Or where you needed to create confusion? Want to exchange petty boredom with excitement? Listen to the Razor.

"There is a dandy little gadget for sale that produces rancid, thick smoke, and it's a Hayduker's dream," says the Razor. "It's called Gopher Gasser, and it creates vast amounts of awful-smelling smoke to chase gophers from their holes."

Obviously this stuff has definite use. While most straight folks use it for rodent intrusion under and through their lawns, I bet you could come up with better applications.

The Razor says the smell is worse than the billowing smoke of a chemical fire. My advice is to shop your local hardware or country feed store and pick up some packs of Gopher Gasser. But, be warned: *this stuff is slightly toxic,* so be careful how and where you use it.

The penultimate odor of burn you never want to smell is that of a large animal, such as a human or cow. A burned one is far worse than a plain, bloated, decaying large animal. Now, if someone could bottle that odor for use against deserving targets . . . any suggestions?

SNAILS

LaMarr Sitzbath, my old foxhole buddy, used to say he'd let a wounded snail drag itself over his raw tongue before he'd marry again. (That's unfair to snails, many of whom have gone on to distinguish themselves in politics). Indeed, Jackie from Clearwater has quite a regard for snails and their acceptable use in today's home decor.

She passes along the idea she used in helping someone —whom we shall refer to as Mark—with some interior decoration. Jackie says, "I loaded some large, slimy snails into plastic buckets and had them secreted into my mark's apartment bathroom. Those live snails really liked the bathroom tile and the damp towels and rugs. It was just precious how they moved in and took over the room."

She says she did the decorating while he was away for the week, and in that time, the little creatures adapted well to their new environment, just making themselves right at home.

That was the substance of Jackie's report. I can only imagine what transpired when the first of Mark's bathroom users visited the new snailatorium. In this instance, I would imagine the smaller creatures had the advantage.

SOURCES

Following are some annotated sources for materials, ideas, products, and persons that have proven to be helpful in the payback business. This is not a universe of sources, but merely a sampling provided by my experiences, experiences of others, plus reputation among experts. My listing these sources does not constitute a Good Hayduking Seal of Approval; these are not endorsements or advertisements. Each listing was current at time of publication.

However, as some companies move, go out of business, or stop communicating with the public, it is possible that you might not get what you want from these listings. You may not even hear back from them. My apologies. In the past, though, the folks I list have proven to be excellent sources. If any of you have sources of your own that you'd like to share with the rest of us, drop me a note: George Hayduke, P.O. Box 1307, Boulder, CO 80306.

Allied Publications, Drawer 5070,
Glendale, AZ 85312.
They list dozens of survival books and manuals that will have definite interest for you. They also sell maps of all sorts and descriptions. Some of their titles will frighten the grown-ups.
Delta Press, Ltd., 716 Harrell St.
El Dorado, AR 71730.
According to my pals in the book industry, these people are one of the most professional, efficient, and easy-to-do-

business-with operations selling books these days. Their catalog is colorful, complete, and easy to use. The catalog itself is worth having; it's like a reference bibliography. I recommend them.

Electronic Surplus, Inc., 1224 Prospect Ave.,
Cleveland, OH 44115.

This is an adult version of Johnson Smith, but with that non-grown-up sense of humor I appreciate. They have just about every electrical gadget and part known to folks who use such technology. They're nice people and totally unstuffy.

The Gas Company, Bowling Green, Box 218,
New York, NY 10274

You gotta have this one. It's wonderful. It is a cassette of real, live human belches and farts. It's fun by itself, but just imagine the Hayduking uses you can get from the cuts on this tape. They're endless. It's only $6.95—well worth it.

Jerryco, Inc. 601 Linden Place,
Evanston, IL 60202.

A gadgeteer's shopping mall between catalog covers best describes these fun folks. I've bought from them for years, for fun and for fun. They are honest, open, and sell quality goodies at very fair prices. Their catalog is written by humans with a sense of humor, a rarity these days.

Life Force Technologies, P.O. Box 4165,
Aspen, CO 81612.

This is the real James Bond catalog. It is full of not-all-that-expensive yet exotic items that amateur and professional Bonds use, including shredders, monitoring devices, security systems, and antisuch systems. Their equipment is real, not replica or toy.

Mail Center of Chicago, 117 W. Harrison,
Chicago, IL 60605.

It is very helpful to have a mail drop. I get a lot of letters asking how to get an out-of-town mailing address. These people will do it for a modest fee. They're solid, professional, discreet, and experienced (since 1944).

Northern Sun Merchandising, 2736 Lyndale Ave., S.,
Minneapolis, MN 55408.

These people are gentle capitalists who sell a variety of posters, t-shirts, bumper stickers, buttons, books, postcards, note cards, etc., of varying parameters of political activism. They're nice people, too.

Photo Kiosk, New London Mall,
New London, CT 06320.

Here is a trustworthy source for discreet, uncensored photofinishing of your private photos. They do disc and 35mm with twenty-four-hour mail turnaround.

SCO Electronics, Inc. 581 W. Merrick Road,
Valley Stream, NY 11580.

I don't know these folks, but they did come highly recommended, and I've seen their catalog. They sell outstanding video equipment, including some very nonstandard stuff that Haydukers could use. They also sell other unusual and useful items.

Square Lake Enterprises, P.O. Box 3673,
Logan, UT 84321.

I've listed these guys for years, as they are good, honest people to do business with. They sell all sorts of highly useful "special effects" chemicals and other pyrotechnical paraphrenalia. They are a good, safe source.

STATUE

Back in the gritty '30s, a statue of Brigham Young was dedicated somewhere in Utah, which is kind of like saying the American flag is flying somewhere in the United States. Anyway, Ray Heffer has a great story here with some very good potential for your use too.

According to Ray, this statue remained under a canvas cover for several days before the unveiling. The unveiling was to be the major attraction for a special day to honor Brigham Young, so a large crowd was on hand.

When the cover was removed, to everyone's shock and horror, some wag had appended with sturdy wire a huge piece of bologna and two brown coconuts in the crotch of old Brigham's statue.

Ray says nobody was ever apprehended and he heard it is still an open case with a reward available. Actually, from what I've heard of Brigham Young, it may have been meant more as a testimonial than a prank.

Perhaps you'll keep this in mind sometime, somewhere when a similar statue is erected.

STP

"YOU'RE FIRED!" are some nasty words, especially when you don't deserve it and the boss is doing it only to cover his own ass. This happened to a friend of Carla Savage, who was fired because she threatened to report sexual harassment.

Carla and another friend used the following method to pay back the boss and his store for the nasty deed. They both went shopping in his variety store, working from shopping lists to make themselves look like serious, real shoppers. Also, they did not acknowledge each other.

"We loaded our carts about half full, then each quietly and unintrusively placed a can of STP at the bottom of the cart. We flicked the pop-top tab back about a quarter inch — just enough to get a thin, steady flow of the syrupy gloop," Carla reported.

"Then we just continued to shop, moving our carts up and down the aisles, laying these thin trails of STP on the floor."

Carla's friend went through three cans; Carla, two. They also visited the section of the store that was carpeted, as well as the deli area. They abandoned their carts and left with a crowd of other customers at lunch time, never to return.

According to Carla, STP is a very nasty stain maker and requires a special solvent to remove it from a tile floor. Carpets have to be professionally cleaned.

SUSHI

It wasn't that many years ago when my fishing friends bought it as bait for tasty game fish. Today, that bait is known as sushi, the edible anthem of what remains of the yuppies and other lovely folks nurtured to the national greed of the Reagan years.

The worm has turned. Apparently, the upsurge in upscale sushi consumption has created a major upchuck of live worms.

It seems that small worms, which infest the krill that fish eat do not die in the fish. Thus, the fish become infested; but they have no symptoms.

Yuppies and other upscale denizens eat these fish, and most will barf out the live worms. Hell no, I am not making this up. I read about it in the *New England Journal of Medicine*. And I am not upset by it in the least. Indeed, I find it amusing.

Perhaps the Yups can buy expensive, exotic new pets— pelican chicks, for example, or other young birds that enjoy regurgitated food. It's called feeding your young.

Or perhaps you can find some Hayduking use for this tasteful tidbit of information. Personally, I can think of some unusual catch-of-the-day to create your mark's own personal sushi. Or perhaps there are some larvae you might add to the mark's store-bought sushi? I'll leave you with the base information. Its use, misuse, or disuse is all up to you. But isn't that what life's all about?

SWEETIES

She wore her makeup like heavy icing on a stale cake. That's when I knew Escobar Retrete, my old Cuban pal from the Alpha 66 days, was in trouble. How do you tell an old friend who thinks he's in love that this woman was to moral larceny what Dick Nixon was to politics?

Eventually, Escobar found out about the other men in "their" bed, the demands for money, and all of the other footprints of this tramp. He asked for help in "doing something." Being a lifelong pacifist, I was the only one among his friends to suggest something nonlethal.

We got a large weather balloon at a surplus store, then waited until he'd moved all of his stuff out of the apartment he paid for (following an emotional, tearful argument) and she moved in the rest of her goodies.

Through surreptitious means, we found out she had a major date that evening. Using a copy of his key that I'd made before he tossed the original in her heavily-trafficked lap, we got into the apartment and laid out the large balloon and filled it with water from the an outside tap. I mean, we filled it up until practically the entire room was taken up with a water-filled balloon.

We all left for the Norte that same day and never came back to see what happened.

Interestingly, as I learned years later on a talk show in Atlanta, Neal did the same thing under similar circumstances. As he explained, "You didn't do anything nasty or bad. That was done by the person or persons who

153

tried to remove the balloon. They are the ones who cause the real damage."

Neal is one of us.

And, as Nester Furringstrip used to say about women, "Even though she's a mighty pretty woman, just remember that somewhere at least *someone* else was already tired of her." Nester's quite the philosopher at the Chambers Hotel bar, you see.

Claude Carpball had a sweetie take him down in a very expensive, nasty way, stealing most of his goods as she moved out of his place and back home with her parents—all while he was at work, naturally. She also began dating a richer fool. Claude bided his time until his sister and her husband announced that he was to become an uncle in seven months. As his sister had a delightful sense of humor, he easily enlisted her in the plan to pay back Sweetie.

Claude's sister went to a Planned Parenthood clinic using Sweetie's name and took a pregnancy test. Guess whose bunny died? When asked who the father was, Claude's sister (a.k.a. Sweetie) acted scared, then blurted out to the counselor that it was her own father. She was an incest victim. She then bolted from the counselor's office and from the clinic.

Can we all guess who the local police called on that very evening? Can we all imagine the confusion, anger, embarrassment, frustration, and irritation that resulted? Meanwhile, Claude and his sister were laughing. I'm laughing. Are you laughing? You should be laughing.

Why is it that some lovely lady who gets married looking like Jamie Lee Curtis takes only ten years of wedded bliss to resemble Don Zimmer with a bad hangover? Or, how did that Dennis Quaid look-alike you married become Burl Ives? Madeline has an answer.

154

Madeline from Phoenix ran across a very rude/crude guy who lied to her big time. One anecdote from her book of payback involved scamming him before he became wise to her knowledge of his activities with many other women, including some nasty date rape with some very young girls.

"I set up a fake date for this jerk, inviting him to a false party at a posh house. He showed up, wrong about everything. As usual, he was drunk and got nasty. The police were called and he got into some trouble."

You say you have a friend, boss, relative, co-worker, or someone else whose spouse or sweetie is playing around without the knowledge of their legit partner? Even if your mark isn't fooling around, you surely can create a lot of trouble for him or her using this stunt anyway. Here's how.

Mr. Big or Ms. Big is on a business trip. You or an accomplice will pose as a travel secretary or some other clerical bureaucrat and call the spouse or sweetie of Mr. or Ms. Big (a.k.a. the mark).

Depending upon circumstance, you will either say that you have the telephone number at the mark's motel or that there has been a change in motels, and you give spouse/sweetie the new number. The latter works better.

Next, you must entice spouse/sweetie to call mark at that number. When the call is made, another of your accomplices will answer the phone and be suggestive, then outraged, and begin to abuse spouse/sweetie, then hang up. If mark is male, use sexy fox female; if mark is female, use husky stud male. Or consider playing switcheroo . . . .

SWIMMING POOL

Trapshooter Lancaster's yard was rapidly turning into a dank, dark, ugly condo for mosquitos and other yucky creatures (i.e., it had passed from being a bog and was now a swamp). The cause was sitting in the next yard, a poorly constructed swimming pool owned by the neighborhood grump, a nasty old fart whose personality would drive a scorpion away. Better yet, his wife, and it was tough to tell them apart, looked like a manhole cover that had been run over by a tank.

These were not only ugly, but *evil* people. They put out poisoned meat in their yard to attract the puppy and kitten pets from the neighborhood.

Well, old Trapshooter fixed that. A friend and he located a very sizeable chunk of pure sodium metal. One dark evening, while Mr. and Mrs. Ugly Bits were squatting around their family pool, our heroes managed to loft the pure sodium metal into their pool.

Trapshooter observed, "I can't say which was more spectacular, the sodium metal hitting the pool or those evil old farts screaming about their pool being on fire. My God, it was just wonderful."

And so it was.

Raymond Heffer used to work with a crew that maintained a pool, and he said kids peeing into the pool was the biggest pollutant. Thus, he always cringed when one neighbor, without a pool, always sent her four kids—uninvited—to the pool of their two little friends. Heffer says the pool parents were too damn wimpy to say anything.

Finally, after two seasons, the nonpool people got their own pool. Ray said, "I thought they should get back a bit of their kids' pee, so one night I visited their pool with an empty urine specimen bottle, plus four bottles of food coloring, three yellow to one green.

"I dumped the food coloring and the empty sample bottle into their pool. The next day, the neighborhood was all stirred up, so to speak. By golly, it did look just like a whole pool filled with pee."

It was not easy getting the pool emptied, cleaned, and refilled, either. But, then, real justice rarely is easy.

TEACHERS

We've all had teachers in school who were brilliant. All you had to do was ask and be prepared to spend the next hour listening to some great pompous bore mouth-farting arcane trivia at you. That's called education. Indeed, I once had a professor who was so smart he could say "horse" in eight languages, yet he rode a cow to work.

One time Ray Heffer knew a very foul teacher who needed to be taught a lesson in humility. Kid Heffer found out from a family friend about a local police sting involving kiddie porn solicitation. The PD advertised kiddie porn sleaze; weirdo people placed orders; police made arrests.

Ray says, "It was easy from that point. I simply used postal money orders and the teacher's name and address to order kiddie porn within the police sting operation. I also placed one order using the teacher's name and the school board president's (who is a real Moral Majority yahoo) address."

There's nothing more to say, Friend Heffer.

TELEPHONES

Although George Bernard Shaw wrote that if one looked hard enough obscenity could be found in almost every book except for the telephone directory, he never knew the crooked businessman who hassled my pal Joe Prosnick. Finally tiring of the asshole mark and the fact that he'd never collect his damages in court, Joe sought collective refuge in the court of revenge.

"This guy had a car telephone and was in an area where he was charged fifty cents per minute for both incoming and outgoing calls," Joe reported. "Through a little ingenuity, I learned his car phone number, which was unpublished, and started to tie up his phone line, sometimes even without his knowledge."

Joe's revenge must have hit financial payoff, as his mark's number was changed the following month. When I last spoke with Joe, he had his sleuths busy on getting the new number. A veteran of this sort of thing, Joe also reminds you to be careful of Ma Bell's security gestapo.

Here are a couple of quickies you can use for laughs while you're planning your next adventure or whenever you want to confuse someone on the other end of the telephone line.

First, you're tired of answering your telephone, or someone keeps calling just to annoy you, or you know it's a telemarketer. When your phone rings, you simply pick it up and instead of saying "hello" or something polite like that, assume your very best bombastic voice and say, "Hi, is

Gerry there?" It works. I've done it. And it's fun. You may have to improvise more conversation if you have a slow caller on the other end, but that's fun too. The main game here is to maintain the attitude that you're the caller.

The second silly stunt is when someone calls you with a wrong number. Or, someone calls your number correctly and you want them to think it's a wrong number. The call could go like this:

Them: "Hello, is this (202) 898-0792?"

You: "No, this is (202) 224-3121."

Them: "Oh no, I know I dialed correctly, I'm never wrong."

You: "Oh, in that case, please excuse me. I must have made the mistake when I answered this call."

Click!

Storm Trooper and his friend Fone Man used their conferencing telephones to gain a measure of payback on a certain fraternity that had been terrorizing the decent folks on campus, as well as on a secondary mark, the timid college president who was too fearful to do anything to stop the drunken violence.

"I called the frat while my friend Fone Man called the college president. When we got both on the line—I had to do a little bullshitting to stall the frat guys while Fone Man got through the president's secretary—and had them conferenced. It was beautiful.

"The frat president identified himself, as did the college president. Just then, I muttered, 'you simple asshole' into my phone. Both parties could hear it. Then Fone Man and I hung up, breaking the conference. Each mark thought that the other had made the call, made the comment, and then hung up," Storm Trooper related with a hearty laugh.

He said they did this a few more times over the next

160

week, until campus security finally raided the frat and things quieted down on campus.

TELETHONS

At one time, telethons were a wonderful way to raise money for good causes, needy kids, local public TV stations, animal rescue, and the like. Lately though, sleazy greedsters have discovered the big-bucks benefits of telethons. Storm Trooper has come up with some ways to do something about greedy telethons and how to involve your other marks in the fun.

"Sometimes I will find an obnoxious telethon and pledge a fair amount of money in a mark's name. Then I call the mark and tell him or her to watch the telethon immediately. When the station people announce the pledges, I bet the mark goes wild," Storm Trooper says.

Another of Storm Trooper's stunts to combat an obnoxious telethon is to call their number and get the name of one of the telethon management people.

"Next, I listen to the next list of people pledging and write the names for the largest pledges. I then call them on the phone and pass myself off as the telethon management person, whose name I use. I badger the hell out of them for more money, trying to be as obnoxious as I can be."

TELEVANGELISTS

I wonder if Mansfield, Pennsylvania, was named after Jayne? I wonder why my old correspondent friend, the Wall, still lives there? Where and why is there a Mansfield? The only thing I don't wonder about is his clever way of dealing with a pod of right-wing religious wackos living close to his place.

The Wall reports, "These mind-thumpers were awful. Nobody in the neighborhood could go outside without them galloping over to verbally and almost physically restrain and then convert you—or if they knew you, to call you a sinner or some other of their nonsensical bullshit.

"They belonged to all the cults—Pass the Loot, the 666 Club, or whatever—and just used to devil us all the time. When I got tired of belching at them, I thought of something more fun."

The Wall waited until the call-in Hot Prayer Line was open, then called the show, which he knew his next door Yahoos watched religiously. Pretending to be their demented son, he reported how he and his little sister were sexually abused and beaten and how their parents made them chew cigars, drink beer, smoke pot, and then (gasp) play cards. He also told the monitor that his parents were getting divorced to spend more time with their boyfriends, and that their parents were an interracial couple.

"We begged for help, guidance, and a visit . . . or for people to pray for us," the Wall said.

Well, as if his prayers were answered, a bit later in that

show the audience and the stars prayed for this very real family with this very real address in this very real town, Mansfield, Pennsylvania.

Some very real shit came down. But the Wall was cool. "I had some out-of-town business when all of that was going down," he related.

It reminded me of the anthem of all of these right-wing fascist-conservative TV preachers who are out for the loot, wrapping themselves in the flag with the Bible held close.

"Jesus loves me, this I know, because the babble tells me so."

TELEVISION

One of Rev. Nasty's relatives was a really evil man who was hated by most of the good folks in the family. Everyone talked, but nobody did anything . . . until Reverend Nasty got tired of the drunken lout who beat his wife, cheated on her, kited his bills, and so on. His major and only joy was getting drunk and watching TV.

"I knew he loved HBO and all of that. I had practiced a lot and could imitate his voice, so I called the cable company in his name and asked to speak to the manager.

"When she came on the line, I really got nasty, crude, profane, gross, and truly rotten. I told her the cable programs were trash, filth, and pornographic. But I also used really crude slang words to talk about her. I also demanded that they come out right away and take away my service or I'd sue, firebomb, and come rip off her clothes . . . ."

Later, Rev. Nasty's sister, the spouse of the louse, told him that the cable people came out that very afternoon and practically tore out the equipment. At first the mark was astonished, then he became angry. He got abusive and the police were called.

The cable company manager filed charges, which the lout denied, but because he'd been abusive to the cable employees, the judge believed the cable lady and slapped him with a major fine, probation, and the threat of a jail sentence for his next escapade.

You have my blessing, Rev. Nasty. Very well done, sir.

If you're interested in noise, please follow the advice of

Carla Savage, who had a friend who used to (key words, *used to*) screw around with the TV remote control to the point of madness.

Carla said, "She drove me nuts, always changing this and that on my set, usually after I had it adjusted the way I wanted it to be. So . . . .

Carla went to her friend's place with a small tube of superglue in her bag. While her friend was busy, and just before Carla left, she cranked the volume of her friend's TV set up to full blast—the set was turned off at the time— then superglued the volume control in the maximum ON, or "SUPERBLAST" position, as Carla calls it.

End of story, as I am sure you get the idea.

TIRES

A neighbor's kid—a gene pool dropout—had repeatedly driven over Calvin's lawn while drunk and mashed his small private hedge. The parents said, "Not our saint-son!" The kid managed to drive away from his mash-the-yard mission, then come back in the other direction and into his driveway with no trace of his yard attack.

Calvin found a fine way to take the air out of the kid's tires, so to speak, *and* put the little rotter into the deep freeze for his dastardly deeds. Showing excellent judgment, Calvin waited several months before going operational. Let the emotions cool and the complaints fade.

"Winter was a few weeks away when I decided what I was going to do," Calvin said. "On a very cold night, with the promise of more frigid weather to continue, I took my portable air tank to a service station *after* I had removed the top valve and poured a quart of water into the metal tank cylinder. I replaced the valve.

"Next, I filled the rest of the tank with air and went to the kid's car late that night. I let some air out of the tires, then adjusted my tank's flow valve so that the air pressure squirted out water, which I put into his car's tires. I refilled them to proper pressure with a bit of air."

It takes a real sense of humor and imagination to enjoy the results of the next day, when the kid drove off in his clunk/clunk ice wagon. Calvin said it didn't really tame the kid until he'd done it three more times. That time, the parents came calling. He said with a hurt expression, "Who, me? I'm a responsible adult!" The blame eventually came to junior and his wild friends. Calvin thought about doing the parental car too, but decided that he *was* a responsible adult.

TRAFFIC

Traffic is one thing that quite possibly has a lower favorable rating than politicians. Maybe. Anyway, thanks to a variety of folks, here are some fun ways to make traffic a more positive experience.

One of the WLW radio traffic reporters in Cincinnati says if you're bothered by a tailgater, a couple handfuls of golf balls tossed out of your window usually discourages these rude folks.

Johnny's former fiancee, who dumped him because he refused to give up playing softball and join her and her parents at the country club instead, was getting married to someone of her own ilk. The reception was being held in her parents' home on a quiet, residential street.

It took work and courage, but Johnny and a couple of pals pulled it off. They borrowed official highway department barricades and detour signs, closed certain roads, and rerouted heavy commercial traffic right down the quiet street where guess who lived and right when guess what was going on.

Johnny, who had a perfect alibi (he didn't need it as it turned out) said that it took police an hour and a half to get things straightened out and get the clogged traffic moving again. In the meantime, the wedding reception was totally ruined.

As a bonus, there were several fender-bender auto accidents, including a police car and the vehicle the newlyweds had been given as a wedding present and were to use for their honeymoon. That incident resulted in a honeymoon delay and an appearance before the authorities. This was an unplanned additional reward, of course.

UNIVERSAL PRICE CODE

The ubiquitous UPC does have a use beyond making supermarket cash registers chirp and chime. Willy from Mesa had some problems with an automatic teller machine (ATM), and the bank humanoids refused to believe him. That's when Willy decided to provide some electronic education.

Bank cards use magnetic tape strips to store the data that are read by the ATM units. Willy wants to know, so he asks rhetorically, "What might happen if you got hold of a secondary mark's ATM card or simply made a plain, name-blank card and glued a UPC strip from a Van Halen tape or a box of 9mm ammunition to it?"

I can imagine some of the things an ATM *would* do with that sort of sensory overload, and one of those would not be to function properly. That's what Willy in Mesa had in mind, I bet.

In his last letter Willy reported that "his" bank has gotten no more human or pleasant to deal with, but that the local newspaper has had some articles about "high-tech mischief and vandalism" on that bank's ATM machines.

My guess is that Willy in Mesa will try harder, as that is the advertising motto of many banks.

URINE

Once in a great while, professional folks (e.g., doctors, dentists, accountants, lawyers) make errors. Mr. Smith was witness to such a happening when a medical-facility person made a mammoth mistake with insurance paper processing, but managed to cover his ass by biting Mr Smith's financial ass. And, as this was a professional signing an official paper that would save them money, the insurance company treated Mr. Smith like the bastard issue of a gypsy moth.

The insurance company wanted to hear nothing from Smith and would pay nothing. The medical facility wanted money from Smith.

"Back then I couldn't afford legal help, and the doctors told me their country-club lawyer buddies would rape me in court, then sue me for slander," Mr. Smith told me.

And here is what else he told me . . . and what he did.

"I went to a sickroom supply shop and bought a catheter, then to a hardware store for some flexible tubing. I attached the flexible tubing to my leg inside my pants and directed the end through a hole slit between the top and sole of an old pair of loafers," he related.

Obviously, Mr. Smith could now relieve himself without using his hands or opening his trousers. Every Friday evening for four weeks, he would go to the medical office to pay a portion of his disputed bill, plus add a little interest of his own.

"I'd fill up on pop, milk, or water after trying not to pee all day. Then I'd go in to pay. While standing there, I would relieve my very full bladder, very copiously, yet quietly, into their thick, shag carpet. On two occasions when no one was looking, I soaked their expensive leather sofa as well."

Mr. Smith says that beer urine is worthless unless you let it ferment inside your body for a day. He advises not to drink a lot of beer. He says to use milk if you're going in freshly loaded.

But, if you can hold your urine or are a regular drunk, then drink beer, but let it build within your system for hours until just before your attack.

"That way, you get that heavy, yellow, smelly urine. That stuff hangs on in a room like a permanent odor spray. It's bad!"

After the fourth week, he noticed professional cleaning equipment in the office complex. After the sixth week, the carpet and sofa had been replaced. Mr. Smith still had seven more payments to make.

And I bet he did.

WATER

If, for whatever reason, you'd like to create some hysteria within the company, institution, or whatever organization with which you are associated, Ray Heffer suggests you play mind games with the water supply. You need an accomplice or two for this stunt.

For a week or so, you and the accomplice start rumors about a possibly polluted water supply. Leave a few forged reports or other dubious documents laying around the office photocopy machines that indicate an investigation of the local water supply is in progress. Locate and clip articles about water contamination and put them up on bulletin boards in the facility. Start rumors with known gossipmongers.

"It's important that you get it started, then drop out of the rumor lead and become one of the mass audience," Ray advises. "Then, after a few days, you're ready for the next step."

That step is for you and your accomplice to visit a few of the restrooms and other water supply areas. With pliers, gently remove the aerator screen assembly from the faucets. Use tape over the faucets if you think the pliers will mar the surfaces.

Place a bouillon cube or food coloring pellet on top of the filter and screw it back on. Every time someone draws water from that tap, it will be brackish in color. If the faucets are the industrial type without aereators, then stick the cube up the faucet and secure it there with screen or a spring-loaded sidebar.

According to Ray, that's all you have to do. The rumor and the colored water will do the work for you. Just sit back and enjoy the harvest of the nasty fun you've sown.

THE LAST WORD

Letters. That's the last word in this volume. Please write. I'm always glad to hear from readers and friends who have ideas, stunts, successes, plans, or funny stories they want to share. Send along questions, too, and I'll try to help in a general advisory way.

If you have something original and hilarious that you want me to use in a future book, please say so. And, if you want me to use a special alias or pen name in place of your real name, please let me know in your letter.

I do answer all of my own mail personally, by the way. I try to be as prompt as possible in getting back to you, but I do travel a lot, so please be patient.

One other thing. Please include your name and return address with each letter, as I don't keep name and address files for friends.

My address is:

George Hayduke
P.O. Box 1307
Boulder, CO 80306